# The *breakup* survival guide for men

## How to Get Over Your Breakup Quickly, Regain Your Confidence, and Move Forward with Your Life

# Susanna Gold

ISBN: 978-1-98-672933-8

2nd Edition
Cover Illustration: Kachaev
Book Cover: Christine's Cover Designs
Createspace, Charleston SC

To my sister Rachel, whose support and opinions were invaluable in the writing of this book.

# Table of Contents

# Introduction

As someone who has suffered from a broken heart, I know the pain of having to carry on when you can't be with the person you love. I had loved and lost over the years, and each time I struggled to recover. But there was one breakup that was far more devastating than the others. After this incredibly painful breakup, I was at a crossroads. I had suffered for nearly a year, unable to accept the end of my relationship. But I knew that if I didn't make a strong and genuine effort to recover, I would continue to be depressed and find little joy in life. I didn't want to become bitter, so I decided to try my best to be positive. It was difficult, but I found that the positive attitude I portrayed on the outside soon became how I felt on the inside. As I struggled to come to terms with my loss, I came up with techniques and solutions that were effective at lifting me out of depression and easing me into my new life without my ex. I would like to share them with you. By learning from my mistakes and remaining optimistic, I was able to get over my breakup and finally meet the right person who I had been searching for most of my life.

If you are struggling to get over a breakup, feeling emotionally drained and as if you might never fully recover, this book will be of great help to you. It offers innovative ways in which to direct your time and energy while rebuilding your confidence so that you will be able to pull yourself out of your negative state of mind, and begin to function again. It will enable you to learn lessons from your breakup, find constructive ways to cope with your feelings, and achieve closure. You will learn how to:

- Accept the end of the relationship.
- Keep yourself from contacting your ex.
- Avoid stress during the healing process.
- Grieve properly and immediately after the breakup so that you don't get stuck in an endless cycle of grieving.
- Analyze and review what happened during your relationship so that you can achieve closure on your own.
- Live in the present and look towards the future instead of obsessing about the past.
- Avoid denigrating yourself and gain your confidence back.

Summaries serve as reminders after each chapter – if you feel the need, you can refer to them whenever necessary. Everyone heals at a different pace. Although the book moves rapidly, don't feel that you must follow a specific time frame. My hope is that you will get to a healthy place emotionally after your breakup, as soon as possible.

**- Susanna Gold**

# Chapter One

## Accepting That It's Over

Breakups are traumatic, life-changing events. When you realize that your relationship is over, it's devastating. There may be moments when you feel sheer desperation. You want her back so badly that the pain is unbearable. You feel helpless because there seems to be nothing you can do to make yourself feel better. You see the world through a gray fog, and it's impossible to concentrate at work or socialize in any genuine way. Everything reminds you of her. Certain parts of town become no-go areas because you went there with her. You attach memories to every store you entered and every restaurant you frequented as a couple. When you do decide to go to these places, memories overwhelm you. You look around; everyone seems to be behaving normally and going about their business as usual. It is a surreal experience because there is a vibrant energy humming all around you, yet you feel like your world has come to an abrupt halt.

You almost feel like a ghost that no one can see, or a victim of an accident who is being ignored. You want to ask people for help, but you know that no one else has that ability - the only one who can save you from your pain is yourself.

When you're alone at home and have time to think, you vividly recall laying next to her, the friends you shared, the world that you built around her. The fact that you miss her and want her back is understandable. However, waiting patiently for a sign from her that she might want to get back together instead of moving forward with your life will only prolong your pain. You could end up wasting months or even years of your life, waiting endlessly for her return. The hope for reconciliation will have you living in a parallel universe - wanting her back while at the same time, wanting to get over her, two conflicting emotions. The only way to get over the breakup is to accept that the relationship is over and make decisions in your life reflecting this.

## Remove the Pedestal

Ask yourself why you are idealizing this person and putting her on a pedestal. What needs did she fulfill in your life? And, why have you been able to recover from past breakups and disappointments, but not this one? Answer these questions and you are on your way to getting over her. Since she is no longer there, it's important that you be able to find a way to fill that emptiness.

Every woman has positive qualities as well as annoying or difficult ones. By telling yourself that your ex was perfect in every way, or worse, that she was "the one," you are imposing your past on your future. Your future is wide open, so don't write off other women or place them in a lesser position in your mind when you are ready to date again. Women are intuitive - when they meet you, if they suspect that you're thinking about someone else and are not fully present mentally, it gives them less incentive to become involved with you.

## Have a Plan

The first few weeks after a breakup are the toughest. Getting through each day is an accomplishment, in and of itself. However, if you know *how* to heal, you can minimize the trauma and drastically cut down on the time it takes to recover. If you set your mind to it, and have some guidance and a plan to back you up, you can get to a comfortable place emotionally and heal considerably in a short period of time. But this can only happen if you have a genuine desire to put the relationship behind you. Instead of stagnating and feeling down every day, you want to feel better. The first step is disconnecting yourself from your ex. This means making the firm decision not to contact her. It takes a great deal of strength to control the urge to see her or speak with her. But the earlier you are able to put the relationship behind you the better it will be for you in the long-run.

# Don't Call Her

It takes super-human self-control not to call her, especially during the first month after the breakup. The problem with ringing her up or instigating a video call with her is this: If you call her you'll be setting yourself back in the healing process – you will be lengthening the time it takes you to get over her. Hearing the sound of her voice would devastate you and watching her speak to you on video would be even worse. The best way to stop yourself from picking up your phone is to view not doing so as self-protection - you are avoiding pain. Delete her contact information from your cellphone so that the temptation is not directly in front of you all day long.

There's a trick of the mind you can use to keep yourself from calling her; I call it the *Seven- Day Layover.* For this method to work we need a hypothetical situation. Let's say, for example, you are going on a vacation, and while in transit you get stranded at an airport in a foreign city because of a storm. Normally, in real life this would only last a few hours or perhaps a couple of days depending on the severity. But for our purpose, let's say it was a total of seven days. You would be unable to reach your destination and to pass the time you would have to think of things to do to keep yourself occupied.

After the seven-day period, you are informed that you can finally catch a plane that will take you where you want to go. Most people would have one of two reactions: They would go on the trip as planned, or they would be so tuckered-out that they would forgo their trip and head back home to recover. Either way, a decision is being made - to go or not to go. You can use the *Seven-Day Layover* scenario to keep yourself from contacting your ex. Here's how: When you're tempted to contact her tell yourself that you'll put her out of your mind for now, but will allow yourself to think about her again in one week's time. You are giving yourself a layover period. During this time remain occupied; keep your normal work schedule, plan lots of activities, and go to all your appointments as planned. Go about life as usual (as best you can). After this period, allow yourself time to miss her and think about her. You might need an hour or even half a day to reminisce about the relationship; looking at photos, listening to music, or watching films that bring back memories of her. But don't contact her! After taking time to do this, find something else to do and remain busy for the rest of the day. After you get through the first week, give yourself another seven-day period. The week after that, do it again. Gradually, the tension you feel will subside each time you put off the call. As time passes, there will be other pressing issues that pop up in your life and it will be necessary for you to direct your attention away from your ex. Before you know it, a month will have gone by, then two, and then three. You'll be amazed at how well this technique works.

## The Social Network and Messaging App Problem

Once you've deleted your ex from your cellphone she will no longer be on the contacts lists of your messaging apps, so her profile photos will stop popping up. You can also set apps in a way that protects you from outsiders accessing your profile if you wish, so that she can't spy on you if you are worried about this. However, social media is more complex and is constantly evolving. Changes to how these sites operate can and do occur on a regular basis due to regulations and decisions made inside of these companies.

When you were a couple, you may have used social networks to interact with each other. The best way to handle these accounts right after a breakup is to make no changes right away. You should never feel pressured into putting your relationship status up on these sites in the first place, but if you wrote that you had a girlfriend, there is no need to change that information now. Walking away from these networks for several weeks until you get your bearings back would be the healthiest thing for you to do. Only pay attention to any social media you utilize for work so that you don't miss out on anything important. If your family and close friends constantly contact you in this manner, ask them to chat with you using other means until you can gather the strength to change your relationship status, delete your ex's photos, and unfriend or block her. Another thing to remember is that you don't have to be corralled into using these sites. If you don't feel that using a particular site is benefiting you, then stop using it. People open these accounts all the time and they also close them.

## The Email Dilemma

If you get a strong urge to email your ex while at work, keep in mind that once an email is sent you can't take it back even if your feelings change later that same day. If you were to get a negative response you would feel hurt, even if you saw it coming. You would be reeling, trying to recover from the blow. Even worse, there's a possibility that you would get no response at all and spend hours or days wondering why, and kicking yourself. To lessen the urge to send her an email, delete emails you've kept on file from her. If you choose, you can block her from emailing you in the future, or if you feel the need, you can delete the email account that she used to contact you on, unless it is work-related.

## Don't Convince Yourself That You Need Answers to Your Questions Before You Can Get Over Her

Rarely will someone give you straight answers or admit the real reason why they chose to end a relationship. Contacting her and trying to get those answers will likely be futile. Short of hiring a private detective, if it was a clear case of infidelity, you will never get the full story. Instead of sitting around feeling desperate, helpless, and wondering *why*, a better thing to do would be to accept that since you won't be getting the information you seek, you will have to get around this problem yourself. You don't need answers directly from her to get over her. You can achieve closure on your own, in your own time, and in your own way. The writing exercise in **Chapter Nine** will help you do that.

## Plan Activities to Keep Yourself Busy

It's important to give yourself some relief from the stress that heartbreak brings. Because all of us experience stress differently, we also have different ways of coping. Becoming involved in various activities and performing simple tasks can help keep you from obsessing about her. If you feel the need, make a list that you can refer to when you are tempted to contact her using different tactics such as:
Diverting your attention, exercise/exertion, and spirituality/looking inward.

## Divert Your Attention

1. Call a friend and talk about subjects other than *her,* and keep the conversation going.
2. Enjoy the company of your friends in person, rather than online.
3. Make some home improvements.
4. Do some basic upkeep on your car.
5. Take on an extra project at work, or work longer hours.
6. Learn a new language.
7. Shop for a better deal: search for a better rate on car insurance, phone service, and other necessities.

8. Go to a bookstore, your local library, or search online for titles that peak your interest.
9. Watch a comedy, action, or horror film (romance is out for now).
10. Update your skills for your job or an outside interest. Take a class or learn on your own.

## Exercise / Exertion

1. Go to the gym and have a workout or sign up for a class such as boxing or judo.
2. Go swimming, play tennis, or try a new sport you've always been interested in.
3. Take a long walk, run, or bike ride.
4. Instead of taking your car for a wash, detail it yourself.

## Spirituality / Looking Inward

1. Listen to your favorite music.
2. Get in tune with nature. Take a walk on the beach or hike up a trail in the woods.
3. Unwind and enjoy your favorite tea or coffee.
4. Spend time with your pet.
5. Buy a gift for a family member or someone special to you.
6. Attend services at your church, temple, or place of worship.
7. Volunteer for charity work. Not only will it make you feel great, but helping the needy will

give you your perspective back. However badly you might be feeling at this time, you'll come to your senses when you meet others whose lives are even harder in comparison.

## Utilize Your Appointment Book

If you keep an appointment book or maintain one in your cellphone, you can use it for more than just keeping track of your schedule. Here's how: If you are using a book, purchase some highlighting pens. Put a highlight marking over the days that you are overwhelmed by the urge to contact your ex. Then, pencil in what set off those feelings and made you consider contacting her. If you are using your phone you can insert text into your calendar so that if you see a pattern you can do something about it. An example might be: During your relationship you used to have dinner together every Wednesday night, and since the breakup you feel particularly lonely on Wednesdays. Instead of feeling horrible whenever that day rolls around, schedule an activity from your list. Go to the gym and get some exercise while spending time in the company of other people instead of being alone, meet a friend for coffee, or ask a friend what films or games he likes, and invite him to come over. Keep trying out different ideas until you find the ones that are most effective at keeping you occupied.

# Vent Your Feelings in Writing

A great way to vent your feelings in a private and deeply personal way is to express them in writing. Writing is especially helpful for people who don't have a close circle of friends with whom they feel comfortable discussing their breakup. If you feel the need, write a letter to her telling her all your feelings. Keep what you've written in a journal and hide it in a secret place or store it on a flash drive. If you don't wish to read it again, tear it out of your journal and throw it away or delete the file at your leisure.

# You've Been Able to Get Through Tough Times in the Past. You Can Do It Again.

Try to recall a challenging period in your life. You may have had health problems, bravely went through treatment, and recovered. Or, you had to pass a rigorous exam, and not only passed it, but scored higher than you ever thought possible. Is there something that you were able to do in your life that others were impressed by, and that you, yourself thought was a great achievement? If so, ask yourself how you did it. If you had the strength and determination then, you can find it now. Try to look at getting over your breakup as another challenge. Yes, it is a different sort of challenge, but it can be met.

# Breakup Survival Summaries

- Oftentimes, the hope for reconciliation is what keeps people from getting over a breakup. So that you don't waste months or even years hoping for her return, start being proactive about healing.
- Take her off the pedestal you've created in your mind. Figure out what needs she fulfilled in your life and fulfill them a different way – start by working on yourself.
- Don't contact your ex in any way; no phone calls, video calls, chats, or emails.
- Delete her number from your cellphone so that you won't come across her profile photo on apps or be tempted to start a chat with her.
- Walk away from your social media accounts for several weeks if possible. Change your relationship status, remove her photos, and unfriend her when you are in a better mental state.
- You don't need answers from her to get over her.
- Think of activities to do that will keep you busy when you get a strong urge to contact her. Base your ideas on what you enjoy and what you think will work.
- Use your appointment book or cellphone to document the days and times you feel the strongest temptation to contact her, and try to figure out what triggers it.

- Express yourself in writing, and get your most private thoughts and feelings out of your system.
- Count your achievements. If you've gotten over large hurdles in the past, you can do it again. Look at getting over your broken heart as another of life's challenges.

# Chapter Two

## Parting with Memorabilia and Dealing with Change

If you have items in your home that your ex gave you or remind you of her laying about, gather them in one place. These are not just objects. To you they have deep meaning and can greatly affect your state of mind. Holding onto these things will cause you further pain and only serve to remind you of what you already know - that you were once committed to this person. If you have the strength, toss them in the trash bin. If you're not quite ready, the second best thing to do would be to place them in a garbage or grocery bag. The purpose of using a garbage bag is not to make light of, or somehow demean memories associated with these things. It's simply the easiest and quickest way to collect everything in one place, and it can be stored just about anywhere in the house. You can stuff it under the bed, throw it in the back of the closet, or place it in a room you rarely enter until you're over the breakup and can dccide what you'd like to keep, and what you want to throw out. If you have photos of her stored on your computer or cellphone, delete them. If you are a sentimental person you might choose to save one photo onto a flash drive and place it inside the bag with everything else. Once you've done this, you might consider some new touches for your home. Make the space where you spend most of your time look different than when you were in a relationship. Some suggestions are:

- Buy some new throw pillows for your sofa.
- Buy new bedding and towels if you attach memories to the old ones.
- Switch around the furniture, buy a new piece, or give away something you don't use.
- Put different artwork up on the walls.
- Clear clutter: get rid of things that crowd your living space or you feel you no longer need.
- Another more drastic option would be relocating. If you've been considering it for a while for various reasons or you have to leave because you were residing at her home, finding a new place to live in a different neighborhood or city might be just the change you need.

## Take Things Slow for a While and Set Your Priorities

Once you begin the process of throwing away her things and redecorating, remember that it's not necessary to finish doing everything in one week or even a month. Move forward at own pace, and if making a change upsets you because you aren't ready for it, then stop doing it and give yourself a break.

You will likely need to slow down your pace in other aspects of your life as well until you adjust to being single again, and no longer have moments when you feel a strong sense of being alone rather than part of a couple throughout the day. So that you can get your errands done and run your life as normally as possible, in the evenings before going to bed each night, write in a journal or on a piece of paper all the things you need to get done the next day. Prioritize the most important things by putting them at the top of your list and place the least important at the bottom. Place your list on the bedside table, tape it to the wall, or on the back of a door. Finish doing whatever you're able to do, and if you are too upset on a particular day to do something, reschedule it for a later date. You *can* do everything that needs to be done, but at a slower pace for now. Accepting this will help you better organize your time and allow you to be gentle on yourself while healing.

## Calming Green

If you're stuck indoors much of the time, for a change of pace consider getting some fresh air outside. Have lunch at a café that has a garden or lush patio. Afterwards, order a coffee and read a book. Or, go for a walk in a park, or on a picnic with a friend. Mellow activities such as this will be helpful at de-stressing you. And a natural, calming environment will help you to get your bearings back.

# Walk Around Your Neighborhood – You Might Find Some Hidden Treasures

If you live in a big city, chances are that there are interesting activities going on in your neighborhood that you probably don't even know about. You don't have to drive a far distance to become more social or at least, find a new favorite hangout to take your mind off your troubles. There might be a wonderful restaurant or coffeehouse close by that you've driven past but never entered, or a gym class offered where you can befriend your neighbors and get in shape at the same time. Instead of ignoring the world right outside your doorstep, take a walk and get to know your area. Walk into every store, check out every menu, talk to salespeople and baristas, take the time to sit in a coffeehouse, and strike up conversations with the people around you. It's important to have face-time with other people because living life online without deeper human interaction will make you feel lonelier and lengthen the time it takes for you to pull out of your depression.

# Take a Trip

A weekend away at a hotel or bed and breakfast is a great way to clear your mind. If you have more time and money at your disposal, taking a week trip or longer is a terrific refresher. It's best to go with a friend so you don't get lonely. Try some new cuisine at the restaurants and enjoy the local culture. Get involved in activities and be adventurous. Take lots of photos –

these can become brand-new memories that have no association with your ex

# Breakup Survival Summaries

- If you have saved mementos from your relationship, either toss these items in the trash, or store them in a garbage or grocery bag until you're ready to decide what to do with them.
- Make changes to your living space so that you are not haunted by memories.
- Delete all photos of her stored in your cellphone and on your computer.
- Take things slow for a while as you adapt to your new life without your ex.
- Surround yourself with greenery and spend some time outdoors.
- Find a place in your neighborhood to go that will help you get your mind off your difficulties, and allow you to be more social immediately.
- Take a weekend trip or longer with a friend so that you can create new memories that are not tied to your ex.

# Chapter Three

## Friends + Time = Recovery

The most important thing when recovering from a breakup is not to be isolated. Hiding away in your home and avoiding people will only make things worse, and lead to a longer, more difficult recovery. Sadness and depression can have a psychosomatic effect, causing you to feel anxious and tired. But being around good friends is the right medicine. Sharing your feelings and letting your friends know your situation will help you both mentally and physically. Because women have the tendency to create support systems and are more open with friends about their feelings than men, they often have an easier time recovering from a breakup, although this is not always the case. Develop your own support system so that you can recover faster.

If you live in a city where you have few friends and family, and only have a handful of acquaintances, choose one or two people who you trust to speak with, and tell them in a diplomatic way exactly how you're feeling and what you are experiencing after the breakup. When you know that there is someone else in the world who understands what you're going through it makes you feel less alone and lessens the pain a great deal.

At this time, avoid being around people who tend to be judgmental or competitive, or spend less time with them. When you're feeling better and regain your confidence you can bring them back into your life.

## Being Discreet in a Work Environment

It's not easy showing a happy face and being productive at work when your heart has just been shattered. If co-workers begin to suspect that there is something amiss, or you feel the need to open up to someone at work, pick one person to speak with who is discreet and trustworthy. When you get your bearings back you can thank this person for their friendship and support by taking him or her to lunch, buying them an appropriate gift, or helping them out in some way.

## Breaking Free from Depression

Not everyone has family or close friends who they feel comfortable confiding in. Some people have a support system, but it isn't enough; they need more help. Seeing a therapist is an option if you feel depressed for an extended period and believe that you're not pulling out of it. If you make the decision to see someone, it can remain a private decision that no one else need ever know about. If you choose to go this route, discuss your options with your health insurer or health service provider. If you aren't covered or the therapist you want to see is in private practice, ask them if they offer a sliding scale payment option to their patients who have difficulty affording regular counseling if this is an issue for you.

It's not unusual for someone to experience extreme emotional trauma after a breakup. Oftentimes, a breakup adds to the number of problems already present in a person's life. This combination of woes pushes them into deeper despair. In rare instances, some individuals contemplate ending their pain in the worst way imaginable. If you feel severely depressed at a particular moment and need to speak with someone immediately, you can. There are organizations located in most countries that are there to help. Some well-known centers are:

- The U.S. National Suicide Prevention Lifeline – (800) 273-8255
- The National Hopeline Network – (800) 442-4673
- Samaritins USA has 400 centers in 38 countries – (877) 870-4673
- Befrienders Worldwide – a global organization.
- Most popular messaging apps and social networks now have suicide prevention tools.

What is most important is that you get your perspective back. Your heartbreak and difficulties will eventually pass, although when you're going through it all you can't always see that clearly. No one is immune to the ups and downs of life. Being able to appreciate the simple things is important. There are so many things worth waking up to every morning, and they matter a great deal. Also, keep your eye on your lifetime goals; you will have something to work towards and look forward to.

## Go Easy on Yourself

- Try to keep daily stress to a minimum.
- Make sure that you exercise and look after your overall health.
- Get plenty of sleep.
- If you have many things to do on a day where you feel extremely down, do your errands and tasks slowly or break them up over several days if they aren't urgent.

After a breakup, it's not unusual for a person to lose confidence in their ability to meet someone new and feel that they are somehow not desirable enough for whatever reason to attract someone they would deem desirable. This is not the case in reality, yet it makes people feel hopeless and depressed for periods of time unnecessarily. Most of us have to go through some difficulties before meeting the right person. You might not have met this person yet, but you will eventually, so try to remain positive and patient.

## Getting Your Sleep

Anxiety caused by a breakup can lead to sleep deprivation. Luckily, there are natural, healthy ways to cope and get your eight hours.

- Respect your body's need for rest and concentrate on pleasant thoughts before bedtime.
- Have a workout whenever possible, except for late at night – this will help you sleep. A brisk forty-minute walk or run around your area is a great way to get in a day's exercise.
- Avoid eating a heavy meal late at night and wait at least two hours before going to bed after eating.
- Drink a cup of warm milk or herbal tea in the evening. Health food stores sell a variety of teas that can be helpful at relaxing you and reducing anxiety such as chamomile, valerian root, and passionflower. These are safe to drink for short periods of time unless you are allergic to one of the herbs listed. Remember to always check labels carefully.
- Avoid caffeinated beverages such as coffee, black tea, or soda late at night.
- If you awaken easily, consider wearing earplugs so that you can get uninterrupted sleep.
- Try to go to bed at the same time every day so that your body adjusts and knows when to sleep.
- Make sure that the temperature in your bedroom is not too warm and that the lighting is comfortable for you. Some people prefer to go to sleep and wake up in a dark room, while others choose to allow sunlight entering their room in the morning to gently awaken them.
- If a particular scent or spice relaxes you, incorporate it into your evening meal or keep it by your bedside. The smell of coconuts might

remind you of a trip you took to the tropics,
or a woodsy scent might make you think of
a cabin in the forest. Allow these scents to lull
you into a relaxed state of mind.

- Reading can help you gradually fall asleep. A
good book can take you to a faraway place and
get your mind off your troubles.

# Breakup Survival
# Summaries

- Avoid being isolated.
- Share your feelings with others and let the people closest to you know what you're going through.
- Seeing a therapist is an option if you don't have a strong enough support system or feel that you are unable to pull yourself out of depression.
- Make sure that you get your sleep. A good workout during the day or early evening will have a beneficial effect on your body and mind and help you sleep. Reading a good book at bedtime is also helpful.

# Chapter Four

## Allow Yourself Time to Grieve

Men tend to put off grieving and have a delayed reaction several weeks or months after a breakup, lengthening the time it takes them to recover. If you wish to avoid this scenario, remember that the earlier you allow yourself to grieve the end of your relationship, the sooner you'll begin to feel better.

Sometimes, friends and family who are trying to help, but don't always understand the circumstances or full extent of the hurt will suggest that you simply, "Get over it." Their intentions are well-meaning, but they are not the ones who are suffering. You can't just magically heal even though you wish you could. You have to go through the grieving process and there's no shortcut or overnight cure. Even if you're a strong and upbeat person it could take months for you to fully regain your emotional strength. Someone who has experienced a loss such as the death of a close friend or loved one, or has had several failed relationships, often recovers more quickly than a young person or a person who has experienced little loss in their life because they are more practiced at dealing with grief.

You will likely feel several different emotions, sometimes all within the same day for many weeks after the breakup. But it's not all bad news because you can find constructive ways to cope with them.

## Disbelief and Denial

It's difficult to accept the finality of a breakup. The first wave of shock comes over you – you can't get your mind around the fact that it's really over. You are used to having her in your life and can't fathom her not being there. Some time goes by and you wonder whether or not you should contact her. You go back and forth with this idea to such an extent that you are paralyzed and can't make a decision about what to do. You find it hard to believe that she hasn't sent you a chat message asking you how you are, or at least done something to let you know she wants to talk. Getting past this confusing time isn't easy. However, there are ways to adjust to the new reality of her not being there anymore: Don't set time limits for her or yourself regarding reconciliation. Don't try and convince yourself that she does or doesn't love you, and don't obsess about how much you still love her. Take the word *love* out of your vocabulary for now. Use your activities list and continually come up with ideas to keep yourself occupied.

# Intense Longing

You long to be with her; you miss the sound of her voice, her scent, her touch. Memories become intensified and emotions run high. You wonder if you will ever feel such feelings again. Holding onto these moments becomes important. If you let them go, you are letting go a part of yourself. But then, you relive the anger and disappointment, and this outweighs the good memories. It's like a roller coaster ride that doesn't stop.

You can gain control of these feelings, but only if you put them into perspective. Consider the longing for her as normal, like the withdrawal someone experiences after ridding themselves of an addiction. When someone wants to lose weight, they can't continue eating junk food. When someone wants to quit smoking, they must stay away from cigarettes. If you want to quit your ex it's best to avoid seeing her, speaking with her, or even hearing about her. Go cold turkey.

# Anger

Anger is one of the bumps on the road in the healing process. So that you don't walk around feeling hostile, it's important that you have a way of dealing with it that's productive and will have a positive effect on your life. The least intelligent thing to do when you are angry about the breakup is to try and teach her a lesson or continue arguing with her. Explaining to her how wrongly or cruelly she treated you will likely be a waste of your time and energy. If you feel that your ex has a difficult personality, is of questionable character, or repeats the same negative behaviors over and over, in the long-run she will suffer because of it. Pointing these things out to her will be futile, as she needs to find out for herself through life experience. She will grow from her mistakes and hopefully change, or perhaps she won't, but that's no longer your problem. Let life unfold as it does and direct your attention towards something that helps you rather than getting riled up over unresolved issues. A better response to anger would be to go to the gym and get into shape. Or, you could go for a long run around your neighborhood when negative thoughts overwhelm you. Do something that allows you to immediately relieve tension.

Remember to avoid alcohol. Drinking is even worse when you're angry than when you're feeling sad. You can lose control and say or do something that you end up regretting. If you're having difficulty controlling anger on a particular day, switch off your phone for a while or set it on silent. Return people's calls when you get your bearings back. You can have a drink with your friends to celebrate once you're over your ex and are ready to meet other women.

## Anxiety

The end of your relationship technically puts you back where you started before you met her – square one. Because you no longer have someone special in your life, you long to fill that void. Some days you feel like you're in a mad rush to meet someone new. On other days, you just want to be left alone and the thought of dating again seems daunting. You have control over many aspects of your life. If you work hard, you have a good chance of being successful. If you study, you will likely earn high marks in school. Dating is a completely different story because relationships are never a sure thing. Breakups cause a great deal of frustration and self-deprecation which can lead to lower self-confidence. Instead of denigrating yourself, continue doing stress relieving activities from your list.

## Feeling Blue

When feelings of sadness overtake you, take some private time, and listen to songs that remind you of her and release your emotions. Sometimes depression causes people to feel tired and slow. If you're having difficulty functioning because you're grieving, go ahead and take a day off from work or leave early. But try not to do this more than once or twice. Your job is important - don't allow the breakup to have such an effect on you that you lose your livelihood.

## Regret

You tell yourself: I wish I had done this or that differently. The shoulda-woulda-coulda trap can keep you up nights. You can't go back in time and undue what occurred and neither can she. Replaying the same scenes in your head and rewriting them like a movie script the way you wish they had played out is pointless. It keeps you living in the past which you can't change.

The one good thing that comes out of regret is that it teaches you about yourself. If you believe that you made a serious mistake, own up to it and accept responsibility, and then make the decision not to make the same error in your *next* relationship. Once you come to your conclusions and make that promise to yourself, don't harp on it anymore.


## You Begin to Snap Out of Your Sadness

You are tired of being depressed. Your mind and body both want you to pull out of it and are telling you so. Your appetite is back, if it was ever gone - some people never lose their appetite. Most likely, you let yourself go while grieving. But now you are beginning to take an interest in your appearance again and want to look your best when you leave the house. You feel like being around people and having fun with your friends. You want to rejoin the world and feel alive again.

# Breakup Survival Summaries

- Allow yourself time to grieve. Don't try and skip this process or rush yourself through it.
- Denial, longing, anger, anxiety, sadness, and regret are some of the many feelings you will experience. Let them play out and find constructive ways to deal with them.
- Eventually, you will reach the point where you don't want to feel down anymore. Your mind and body will come to a consensus and you'll want to rejoin the world.

# Chapter Five

Keeping It Together

## Don't Let Curiosity Get the Best of You

Where is she going? What is she doing? Who is she with? These are questions that can eat at you non-stop. The temptation to drive by her home or workplace in hopes of catching a glimpse of her can be overwhelming. The mystery of not knowing about what's happening in her life makes her seem unobtainable and desirable. Because you are not communicating with her, you can't simply contact her and ask her what she's been up to, so you invent all sorts of scenarios in your mind. You think to yourself: Maybe she's already found someone else. You imagine her going out at night with her friends and meeting other men. Or, you are concerned that other men are coming across her profile somewhere online or on dating sites, finding her attractive, and contacting her.

An overactive imagination and directing your energy towards this frame of thought is counterproductive. And driving by her home or workplace to see if her car is there or the lights are on doesn't give you much information about what's going on with her. In actuality, things are probably pretty much the same. The only difference is that you're no longer in her life.

It might be true that an attractive woman has an easier time meeting men than the reverse. However, quantity is not quality. Most women are protective of themselves and cautious as a general rule. Maybe your ex attracts attention, but that doesn't mean she will become romantically involved with any of her admirers.

## You Accidentally Run into One of Her Close Friends

One of the most awkward and dreaded situations is crossing paths with an ex's close friend in person or online. The first thought is almost always to duck and run, but then other ideas pop up and you consider your options. You might think: Should I just say hello like a normal person? If I pretend that I didn't notice her would it look natural? Could I get away with subtly questioning her to find out if my ex is seeing someone?

Remember that this person is your ex's friend, not yours, and she will do and say what she feels is in the best interest of her friend. There's no harm in saying a polite hello and asking her what she's been up to lately. You can also share some basics about what's been going on in your life. But avoid going into the whole spiel. Your life is your business and if you don't want to share you don't have to. If she volunteers information about your ex, then so be it. But don't delve further or prompt her for more details – it's not healthy to go on a fishing expedition. If you dig too deep, you might find out something that hits a nerve. Avoid having your buttons pushed, and in this instance, protect yourself *from* yourself.

## Try Some New Hangouts

You don't have to stop going to your favorite restaurant or pub because there is a possibility of running into your ex if you were regulars as a couple. But it's probably a good idea to stop by at an hour when you know she's least likely to be there, at least until you're in a stronger place emotionally. Now is a great time to try some new places where you don't have memories trailing you.

## Don't Search Online for Information About Her

It's not uncommon for someone recovering from a breakup to become curious about what their ex is doing. To alleviate this, they will search for information about them online – the most obvious place to look is at their social media accounts, if they have any. If they see that their ex's relationship status has changed or a photo of her with a new man, they will then check his profile page to find out more about him. But connecting the dots can be challenging and on some sites an obvious trail is left behind. If this describes what you've been doing, break the pattern and stop tormenting yourself. Using social media for this activity is mentally taxing and checking these accounts can lead to an unhealthy obsession, keeping you from moving forward with your life.

Keep in mind that no one's life is frozen in time – things happen to people constantly such as career changes, marriages, divorces, weddings, funerals, and travel. You are no longer in her life and she is no longer in yours, so none of the people displayed in the photographs on her profile page should be of relevance to you. Watching her life unfold as an outsider is pointless and a complete waste of your time. Instead, spend your time creating a better life for yourself and leave her in the past where she belongs.

## Messaging Apps and Your Ex

The only way that you can see your ex's profile photo on a messaging app or when she last used the app is if you keep her number in your cellphone. Her "last seen" or "last online" status doesn't really tell you anything about her life, only when she last used the app. If her "last seen" was at 3 a.m., it doesn't necessarily mean that she stayed out all night with a new love interest. It might mean that she sent a message to her mother overseas who lives in a different time zone. This is why it's imperative that you remove her number from your phone.

# How to Handle a Situation Where Your Ex Has a Publicist

If your ex works for a high-profile company, is a well-known person, or a member of an affluent family, you might come across information about her online that pops up unexpectedly. Stories about VIP's and their family members are spun by public relations machines, so don't believe the spin. Everyone at some point suffers trauma and setbacks in their lives, but a good publicist is skilled at keeping those details hidden. What's written for public consumption is often sheer fabrication. You might read that your ex is dating a good-looking, successful businessman. However, in reality she hardly knows him and just happened to be standing next to him in a photo for a fundraiser. And even if they did end up dating and getting married, few celebrity marriages last very long. There's no point in making yourself upset over something that either isn't true or won't stand the test of time, so avoid the temptation to read these articles.

# Don't Try to Be Her Friend

When you're vulnerable and hurt it makes no sense to hold on to the source of pain. Your life might feel empty without her while you're adjusting, but attempting to fill that void by turning your ex into a friend will only slow your progress in getting over her. Even worse, it keeps you living in the past. It also gives you the horrible feeling of being demoted. If you have a strong desire to hold on to her as a friend, ask yourself if your true motive is to get close to her so that you can win her back. If she began dating other men and chose to discuss those relationships with you, would it get under your skin? Be honest with yourself – most likely it would. When you are no longer emotionally invested in her, you might choose to be her friend. Until that time, it's foolish to think that being her buddy will have a positive influence on your life.

## Are You Flirting with the Idea of Getting Back Together with Her...for All the Wrong Reasons?

Our lives are multi-dimensional. We have our careers, we socialize with friends and family, and we have romantic relationships. When one aspect of our life falters, it's only natural to try and offset that loss by directing our attention towards other things that are going well. For example: If you dislike your job, but you have someone to come home to who you have a secure and happy relationship with, the enjoyment of your job on a daily basis is less vital to your well-being. Whereas, if your relationship ends, but you have a job that is rewarding and a group of supportive friends whose company you enjoy, it will be easier for you to accept a romantic loss.

If you're feeling lonely and as if things haven't been going your way lately, it's probably a good time to make some changes. If your job isn't leading you in the direction you want, consider getting into a field that you find more interesting. Join clubs, network with colleagues, and socialize more in order to make new friends if your old ones are too busy to spend time with you or have drifted away. By improving other areas of your life and setting your sights on your goals, the breakup will hold less significance.

## Believe It or Not, Having to Pay Your Bills is a Godsend

The first concern of most people is to keep a roof over their heads, as well as put food on the table, and pay their bills. At any point in life this can mean working extra hours, taking on another job, starting a business, or going back to school. When most of your time is taken up with concerns of survival, you can't sit around thinking about your ex. You have to plot out a strategy to remain competitive and reposition yourself in preparation for changes up ahead. The grit of life is enough to tear you down. However, after a major disappointment it can be your saving grace. Time really does the trick. The harder you work and the more responsibilities you have, the quicker it flies. One day, many years from now, you may come to view your past in blocks of time. You'll remember that you once worked for a certain company, and at that time you were dating so-and-so, and the relationship ended.

Always remember to count your blessings. There are things you have that others don't, be it your good health, a caring family, a good job, or enough money in the bank. If you're grateful for what you *do* have you won't pay so much attention to what you don't.

# The Wisdom of Strangers

If you think you've been having a rough time lately, think again. When you open up to strangers, you'll find that you're not alone. Personal dramas you'll hear from ordinary folks will blow you away. These conversations can take place online, or you might be on a plane for a few hours and get seated next to a friendly, talkative person. Or, maybe you'll end up sitting on the subway next to someone for a long ride. Try striking up a conversation once in awhile. If you open up first, that person might share their experiences too. It's often helpful to get the opinion of someone who is a complete outsider. They might have some good advice and a different take on life.

# Breakup Survival
# Summaries

- Don't waste your time and energy checking on your ex's comings and goings from her home or workplace.

- If you run into one of her friends, simply be polite. If she volunteers information about your ex that's her prerogative, but avoid the temptation to wheedle information out of her.

- If you have a favorite restaurant or hangout and your ex likes going there too, you should still go and enjoy yourself. However, you might consider going at an hour when it's unlikely she'll drop by until you're over her. You should also scout out new places.

- Don't look up your ex online to see what she's been up to lately. Doing this can lead to an unhealthy obsession.

- Make sure that you've deleted her number from your cellphone so that you aren't tempted to check her "last seen" status on an app that you know she uses. This information will only tell you that she is using the app regularly. It will not give you an accurate depiction of what's happening in her life.

- Don't try to be your ex's friend. It will keep you from fully getting over her because she will still have a role in your life.

- You can have a full life with or without being in a relationship by having a career you find satisfying, and friends whose company you enjoy.

- Most of us have to work hard to get by every day. The more responsibilities you have, the quicker time flies. And as time passes, the hurt goes away too.
- If you think that life has been tough lately, try opening up to strangers. It's likely their stories will be even more harrowing than yours. Sharing your experiences with a complete outsider will give you a fresh perspective.

# Chapter Six

## Avoid Comparing Your Life to the Lives of Others

When you walk around town after a breakup, couples seem to stand out more. You never paid much attention to them before, but now, suddenly they're everywhere. You feel a visceral response when you see them holding hands and looking blissful – you're alone, and these people have someone. Try not to see the world as a place where you lose, and others win. What you see when you look at a couple is a picture frozen in time. They appear to be happy at that moment, and they are together on that day. Whether or not they remain a couple is an unwritten story, and unless you know them personally you'll never know the ending. And although misery loves company, in your heart you probably wish them well.

Looking at the social media pages of others can have an even worse effect on a person's psyche because people use these sites to promote themselves or entertain an audience. What you see on social media is not a genuine portrayal of a person's life.

They are displaying a sugar-coated version, and sometimes what's posted is completely fake. When someone is skilled at self-promotion, they can make others believe that they have it all when they don't. So, don't ever compare yourself to these fraudsters, and don't let the narcissistic tendencies of others affect how you feel about yourself. Detoxing from social media and cutting yourself off from all the nonsense is often the best thing to do.

It's best at all times, not just while recovering from a breakup, to avoid comparing your life to the lives of others. It's easy to envy people who you believe have a better life and what appears to be a good relationship. However, since you are on the outside looking in, you really don't know whether the person you envy or admire is happy, or has the life that they want. You don't know what's going on in another person's mind or how they view their current situation. The person you envy might secretly envy you. There are plenty of people who are disillusioned and disappointed in their relationships. People can feel lonely even surrounded by a large circle of family and friends.

No one can predict what will happen in the future. The unexpected always pops up in people's lives, be it good or bad. Complete reversals of fortune are commonplace in this world. Look upon this time when you find yourself single again as a period in which you have the opportunity to do things you wouldn't be able to do if you were in a serious relationship. And remember, although you might be feeling lonely now because of the breakup, these feelings and your current situation will not last forever.

A positive way to view the lack of romance in your life at any given time is to tell yourself that you would like to have romantic love, but that you don't need it to feel complete. Romantic love will come again when you're in a good state of mind and are open to it. You can't always force it to come when you want it unfortunately, but with or without it you can enjoy life. There are other forms of love too – they might not be the romantic kind, but they are also wonderful; the love you give and receive from close friends and family, the passion for a career you've chosen, and the love for a sport or hobby you're good at. Life is not empty without romance, not by a long-shot.

When you feel happy in your own skin, you are never lonely. You have friends, hobbies, and interests that keep you busy and satisfied. Having a woman in your life is fantastic, but not having one doesn't mean that you can't enjoy your life to the fullest. You will meet someone else, but in the meantime, don't obsess about not having someone. Realize that being single is okay. People find themselves single for all sorts of reasons and this can happen at any stage of life.

## When the Feelings Are Right but the Timing Is Off

All over the world, millions of men and women meet each other every day and begin dating. But personal issues and outside pressures influence each person's openness to commitment. People's needs and desires change constantly, and when a couple succeeds it has a lot to do with a meeting of the minds. Sometimes two people are right for each other, but the timing is off. There are all sorts of things that can happen in a person's life to make them unavailable for a relationship. It can be personal or financial difficulties, family or work pressures, a desire to reach their goals, or a lack of maturity, meaning the person doesn't know herself well enough to know what she wants in life. The tragedy of bad timing is that there's nothing you can do about it. The only way to handle the situation is to go on with your life - date other women and put the relationship behind you. It's possible that if you and your ex had met at a different time in your lives the relationship would have had a better chance of survival due to any number of reasons. So, if you feel it's applicable, you can place some of the blame on timing.

Oftentimes, the fact that a relationship fails is a blessing and it's for the best in the long-run that it ended. You'll look back later in life and realize how lucky you were that you had the time to travel, start a new career, or meet the *real* love of your life. When you meet the right person, you'll know it and so will she. This woman won't allow outside pressures to get in the way of being with you, and the timing will be right.

# Breakup Survival
# Summaries

- When you envy or admire someone, you are on the outside looking in. That person might not feel lucky and fulfilled in their life. In fact, they might feel that you have it better than they do.
- A lot of what people post on social media is exaggerated or even fake. Don't let other people's need to pretend that they are on top of the world, when most likely they aren't, affect your psychological state. Don't waste your time comparing yourself to these people because most of the time you will be comparing yourself to a bogus creation.
- Learn to be comfortable in your own skin whether you're single or in a relationship.
- Sometimes the success or failure of a relationship has a lot to do with timing. If you feel that bad timing played a role in your breakup, there's nothing you can do about it now. Accept that it was a contributing factor, and move on.

# Chapter Seven

## Reward Yourself and Improve Your Mood

It's not easy letting someone you love go, let alone someone who you were close to on a physical level. After some time has gone by, the gray fog around you will lift a little bit at a time. While this is happening, do whatever is necessary to cheer yourself up. Ask yourself this question: What are the things that make me happy under normal circumstances?

If you enjoy skiing and it's the right season, you could invest in some ski gear that you've always wanted but weren't willing to spend money on before. Once you're properly equipped, you can fully experience the thrill of rushing down the mountain. If you like to work on your car, buy some of the parts you've been dreaming about getting. If you've needed a new laptop or cellphone for a while but have been putting off buying one, now is a good time to do it. Treat yourself in ways that you are certain will make you feel good and improve your life. However, before you go out and start dropping cash, assess what you can and can't afford. There's nothing wrong with buying on a whim, but make sure it's not a big-ticket item unless you're confident that it won't put a dent in your finances.

## Exercise

Exercise is the most effective anti-depressant in the world; it truly lifts your spirits, naturally. In the short-term, if you start an exercise routine you'll feel better emotionally, but in the long-term if you keep it up you will be in better condition physically than before the breakup. You'll want to look your best when you start dating again and having a firm physique will give you the extra confidence you'll need to approach women. If you don't want to join a gym, you don't have to. You can buy some weights to use at home and jog around your neighborhood. Becoming more active also gets you out of the house so you stop moping in your spare time.

## Update Your Wardrobe

Going through your closet and deciding what you like to wear and what you don't need anymore will give you an in-house project to help keep your mind off your ex. Set aside clothes that you never wear and put them in a pile. You can sell these items online, or they can go to a thrift shop or local charity. Getting rid of old or unworn clothes clears clutter, and giving certain items away allows you to shed memories of the recent past.

Now is a good time to update your wardrobe - this can be as simple as buying a couple of new shirts, jackets, or pairs of shoes that are the latest style. Make sure that whatever you buy is well-cut - women appreciate a man who wears clothing that is stylish and flatters his build, and when you're dating again this will be important. If you're disinterested in fashion altogether, keep in mind that you don't have to be super-fashionable, but your style should be current.

## Avoiding the Pizza and Beer Binge

It's important to eat right and stay healthy even when you want to eat two whole pizzas in an attempt to self-medicate yourself out of depression. It's not a good idea to use food as a pick-me-up because it can become habit. But after a devastating breakup, you can cut yourself some slack. It's not breaking your diet if you treat yourself to two decadent meals a week so that you will have a guilty pleasure to look forward to that will temporarily relieve stress and anxiety. But only allow yourself this treat if you have a strong craving for a rich meal. Don't do it for the heck of it. The idea is to give yourself some leeway during a down period in your life, not overeat and make yourself ill (nausea would defeat the purpose), or pack on pounds. Set a time limit so that you don't gain weight – for most people two or three weeks is reasonable. You might choose to be mindful of your health by using substitutes as satisfying alternatives. Instead of having a dinner of barbecued ribs, wedge cut fries, and a slice of cake for dessert, have a salmon steak with vegetables, and fruit for dessert with a bit of chocolate sauce drizzled on top.

## Some More Mood-Lifting Ideas

Look forward to something that you rarely treat yourself to such as a concert or sports event. If the weather permits, go to the beach or a park over the weekend with friends, get some sunshine, and play a sport you enjoy. If you want to unwind but aren't in the mood to be social, make of list of films you'd like to watch or music you'd like to download. When you find the time, watch your favorite films and enjoy the music you've put off listening to because you were busy or feeling down. While doing this, remember to switch off your cellphone. You are taking a badly needed break, so spend some quality time by yourself, doing exactly what you want to do.

## Quiz

How do you think your recovery is going so far? Have you had a set-back and contacted your ex? Has rewarding yourself, exercising, and keeping yourself distracted made you feel better? Answering these questions will help you assess whether or not you're on the right track. Circle your answers and tally up your score:

## 1. When you got the urge to contact your ex recently, how did you handle it?

a. I gave her a call because I needed to speak with her so that I could get my stuff back and clear some issues.

b. I sent her a chat message and asked her how she was doing.

c. I added her number back into my phone and spied on her through messaging apps.

d. I exercised and then called a friend.

## 2. When you were sitting at home alone in front of your computer the other day and she popped into your mind, what did you do?

a. I checked her social media page using a fake account.

b. I searched several dating sites, checking to see if she was a member.

c. I composed a chat message but decided not to send it.

d. I concentrated on what I was doing and put her out of my mind.

### 3. If you saw your ex's mother at the grocery store what would your reaction be?

a.  I would pull her aside and attempt to wheedle information out of her about her daughter.
b.  I would suddenly become nervous and leave the store.
c.  I would duck behind the avocados and pray that she didn't see me.
d.  I would acknowledge her with a polite hello if I crossed her path and then go about my shopping.

### 4. When members of your family who took a liking to your ex inquire about her, what is your response?

a.  I'm not speaking with certain relatives at the moment because they keep talking about her.
b.  I raise my voice and tell them, "Enough already!" and leave the family party early.
c.  I tell them that I once deeply cared for her, but unfortunately, the relationship couldn't be salvaged.
d.  I explain to my family that it's over and they should accept it.

**5. When you came across a photo of her that somehow survived the purging process, what did you do with it?**

a. I saved the photo on my cellphone.
b. I directed my attention elsewhere, but I didn't delete it.
c. I downloaded it onto a flash drive, placed it with my stash of "ex-stuff," and put it in a place where I wouldn't come across it.
d. I deleted it.

**6. On days when you're feeling especially down about the breakup, what do you do?**

a. I leave work early, go home, eat an entire pizza, and mope around.
b. I go to work and return home, but that's about it. I'm not ready to socialize or get back to my normal life.
c. I call a friend who will listen and talk about how I'm feeling.
d. I finish my workday, have dinner, relax awhile, and then exercise. Afterwards, I watch a movie I've been looking forward to seeing.

## 7. On the days you've chosen to spoil yourself, what action do you take?

a. I decide that it's pointless. Nothing makes me feel better.
b. Although I've set aside some money, I haven't gotten around to treating myself because I've been too depressed.
c. I know what I want, but I haven't gotten around to picking anything up in my free time yet.
d. I've worked out a budget and treat myself when the urge takes me.

## Let's See Your Score:

**A's = 1 point**
**B's = 2 points**
**C's = 3 points**
**D's = 4 points**

## 7-12 points:

You are still in the beginning stages of the grieving process, so go easy on yourself. Avoid being isolated and call your friends regularly. You might want to have a friend contact you at different intervals of the day to check up on you until you're feeling better. As you heal you will go through different stages of grief, and you'll lean on friends less and less as your recovery progresses.

## 13-18 points:

Getting over your ex is a struggle for you, but at the same time you are able to come to terms with the end of the relationship. Spend more time with supportive people and think of new activities that would be more effective at keeping you focused on things other than her. Make sure that they are right for you and that you will really do them.

## 19-23 points:

You have your confidence back, are functioning at full capacity, and are optimistic about the future. Some days are harder than others, but you can handle it.

## 24-28 points:

Your recovery is coming along brilliantly - whatever you're doing is working, so keep it up.

# Breakup Survival
# Summaries

- You've suffered through feeling blue and fighting the temptation to contact your ex. Reward yourself for those accomplishments.
- Treat yourself to some things you've always wanted but put off buying in the past, and plan some fun activities. However, remember to keep an eye on your budget.
- Exercise to keep fit and alleviate depression.
- Update your wardrobe and give away clothing that you no longer wear.
- Quiz yourself on your progress. If you are still in the early stages of grieving after several weeks have passed, go easy on yourself. Continue to exercise regularly and think of new activities to do that will help you keep your mind off your ex.

# Chapter Eight

## How to Handle an Ex Who Is Still in Your Life

### You See Your Ex Every Day at Work

The slow-developing romance that occurs between two people who work together, enjoy each other's company, and realize that they want to become involved romantically often leads them to the altar. But when an office romance goes sour, it can make for an incredibly sticky situation. If you find yourself in this quandary and you're dreading going to work, keep your chin up – there are ways to deal with it. During the awkward stage immediately after your breakup there are a number of things you can do to make your situation more tenable:

1. Talk to her in a polite, respectful manner. Tell her that since your jobs and reputations are important to you both, you have no option but to show a

classy face to your co-workers and get along in public.

2. Anything that the two of you feel you need to talk about can be discussed after work and away from the office at a neutral location such as a coffeehouse, or over the phone on your own time. It's a good idea to keep these discussions face-to-face and not use messaging apps because sometimes people keep records. Conversations that take place through apps are often more casual than people realize and can give a bad impression to outsiders.

3. Never use company email to discuss private issues. Under certain circumstances these emails can be accessed if the company you work for chooses to view them.

4. Take on work assignments that she's not directly involved in if you have that option until things cool down.

## Display Confidence at the Office

The most masterful way to handle an uncomfortable office situation is to simply do your work and avoid looking disheveled or distraught. Since people are judged by their competence, behavior, and reliability on the job, co-workers will respect you and will be less likely to take seriously any rumors that might be circulating if you simply continue to behave normal

If you and your ex are able to pull through this situation unscathed and possibly even be comfortable working with each other again, you've truly accomplished something. The name of the game is to keep your job - and your sanity.

## You See Your Ex on Campus

A college campus appears to be a massive, sprawling place at first. But when your ex attends the same school it suddenly feels a lot smaller. Is there a coffeehouse or hangout that you and your ex both regularly visited when you were dating? What would you do if you were to walk inside to get a cup of your usual blend, and you ran into her standing with a group of her friends? Here is a suggestion: Remain outwardly calm, even if your heart is pounding so hard that you think others can hear it. Say a polite hello if you have to walk by her and your eyes meet, or give her an acknowledging nod if there is distance between the two of you. Order your coffee, and when it's ready head out the door. There is no need to speak - your body language can speak for you. Send her the message that your world has not been shattered. Give her the vibe that you are busy with your studies and have to get to class or write a paper that's due soon. That's the purpose of going to school in the first place. Your ex knows this because she's working towards the same goals. Accepting the fact that you might bump into her once in awhile will help you adjust. Relax – she's an ex-girlfriend. How many people on campus have an ex roaming around? I'd say the percentage has got to be pretty high. You're hardly alone.

# You Run in the Same Social Circles

When a relationship ends, friends that you made as a couple are stuck in the middle. They have to think carefully about which one of you they are going to invite for dinner or join them for an event. Usually, people sympathize with the person who was mistreated and gravitate towards them. However, there are no assurances for the one who suffered most because a talented manipulator can sway the crowd in their favor. Oftentimes, after a divorce or a long-term relationship ends, people lose longtime friends causing them to feel abandoned. People who you were both close to might decide to stay away until things have calmed down, while others you might have to write off. Friends that you made as an individual, who had little or no contact with her will most likely remain loyal.

If you lose some friends after the breakup, there are many ways you can look at the situation, and believe it or not, not all angles are bad. One immediate benefit is that you can now pick and choose friends based solely on whose company *you* enjoy, and no longer consider what activities she liked, and whose company she preferred. During your relationship, you may have attended parties or regularly had dinner with people you didn't particularly care for. Well, lucky you – you don't have to see them anymore.

Most people categorize friends, although they might not be aware of it. There are those who you keep close to you as trusted confidantes, some are acquaintances who you see occasionally, while others are on the periphery of your life. The best way to handle a loss whether it's temporary or permanent is to do a reshuffling of friends and try to make new ones. If you'd like to do a reshuffling, here are some suggestions: The first thing you should do is reach out to the friends who you suspect are no longer going to be a part of your life because your assumptions about them might be incorrect. A couple that hasn't called you in a month may have gone on an extended vacation, lost a loved one close to them such as a parent, or simply wanted to take a break from socializing. You'll never know unless you contact them. Next, think of an individual who you've always liked but never spent time cultivating a friendship with because most of your time was taken up when you were in a relationship. This person may be either in the acquaintance category or even on the periphery of your life - it doesn't matter. Get in touch with them and suggest you meet for lunch, or take part in an event or sport. If they have the time and the activity you suggest piques their interest, they might decide to set aside a day to spend with you. That day could lead to a friendship that is healthier and more valuable than the ones you lost.

# Breakup Survival Summaries

- If you work in the same office as your ex, suggest being civil since you both value your jobs.
- If you have issues to discuss, this can be done after work at a neutral location or over the phone.
- Avoid using messaging apps when discussing your breakup. Viewed by others, these chats can paint a negative picture of your character that is inaccurate.
- Continue to prove your competence at work; don't let the breakup jar you.
- If you are a student and attending the same college as your ex, although it's tough, remember that the purpose of being at school is to attend classes and study so that you will have future opportunities in life. This should be your main focus.
- If you and your ex run in the same social circles you may lose friends after the breakup. This might be permanent or temporary. If you lose a friend or two, don't obsess about getting them back. Instead, try to make new friends by socializing more and reacquainting yourself with the people you already know.

# Chapter Nine

## Achieving Closure

Closure happens when you believe that you know the fundamental reasons why the relationship ended, and you don't want or need to rehash what occurred. It is the equivalent of saying to yourself: "My relationship is over, and I know more or less why. And it no longer matters. It's time to let go and move on." But unfortunately, not everyone is able to do this. Sometimes, people ignore warning signs that things are going badly while in a relationship and remain in denial until the very end. This makes it harder for them to fully let go.

When a person is in love they look for the good in their partner and rationalize away negative behaviors. They are so busy looking for positive signs that they often miss the obvious. This is one of the main reasons that after a breakup, people are left feeling confused. If this represents you, you might consider doing an analysis of the relationship through a writing exercise. The main purpose of this exercise is for you to reach an epiphany that ends your confusion. You will no longer have unanswered questions haunting you.

It's that moment when you say, "Aha! That's why things unfolded as they did. I now feel that I know all I need to know. I can finally let go."

Let's begin the closure process by looking at your ex's personality and behavior. Write down all the good things about her personality. What were the qualities that drew you to her and held your interest? What made her special or different than other women you've dated? What were the defining moments when you felt that she was the right person for you? This can be titled List #1. Underneath that paragraph or series of bullet points (however you choose to organize your thoughts), write what you disliked about her. Be honest in your evaluation. Don't give credit where it isn't due, and don't demonize her either - simply state your perspective. Remember, this list is solely for you. You won't be showing it to anyone else.

Pull up another blank page and title it List #2. Write down what you feel your ex did to improve your relationship, and what she did to harm it. Under the "Improve the Relationship" category, some examples might be: She went out of her way to be kind to your friends and family. Or, maybe you trusted her and never felt suspicious or wondered where she was; the relationship ended because of reasons other than infidelity. Under the "Harm the Relationship" category, write what you feel she did that was destructive and hurtful to you. It takes two to build something together, but it takes one or several actions by one or both parties to irreparably damage it and bring it to an end.

In a new paragraph, write what *you* did to make the relationship better, and what you did that was wrong.

Underneath that, write down what the relationship dynamics were. Do you feel that the relationship was a healthy one? Were arguments resolved? Were either of you bored with the relationship or not put enough effort into it? If you were to compare your relationship to a musical piece, would you say that it was melodious or off-key?

Now, make a third list - List #3. Write down the clues that indicated something was seriously wrong and made you wonder if the relationship was salvageable. What were the definitive moments and series of events that occurred? Couples break up because they can't get past an issue – what was it? This list is the most important because it describes the downward spiral that led to the end of the relationship.

Once more, pull up another blank page and title it List #4. Write down how the relationship ended. Was it abrupt or drawn-out? Did you believe that she was unfaithful to you? Did you leave her because you were unhappy and had little optimism that things would get better? Did she walk out on you? Did she pull a disappearing act and cut off communication? Write down what occurred that brought the relationship to its final end.

At the end of this writing exercise you should have a better understanding of yourself, your ex, and why the relationship ended. Hopefully, you will have an epiphany while making your lists, but if you don't have it now, it will come eventually. It might happen unexpectedly while you're driving or doing something you normally do every day. You'll come to important conclusions and say to yourself: "My confusion has ended." You'll finally be able to connect the dots and mysteries will unfold automatically. Keep these four lists handy so that you will be able to find them should you ever feel the need to refer to them.

In addition to your lists you can help yourself further by recording your feelings and suspicions about what happened during your relationship privately throughout the day on your cellphone recorder. Some people even prefer making voice recordings over lists, although doing both is by far the most helpful. Playing them back to yourself when you find the time will aid you in reaching important conclusions.

## Feel Good About Having Been Hopeful

Hope is what propels the human spirit. No invention would ever be discovered, and no one would venture out into the world if they didn't have hope. The fact that you invested so much of yourself in another person is a wonderful thing. You experienced the freedom of allowing someone to enter your world and share your life. Endings are always hard; the finality of it and the fact that the person is no longer available are both devastating. But you had this person in your life and enjoyed what she had to give and teach you. She also learned from you. You had shared experiences which you can draw lessons from. If you'd like, light a candle in honor of what the relationship meant to you, and to mark the end of it. Cherish the good memories. And most of all, be proud that you were hopeful.

# Improving Your Self-Esteem After Rejection

All human beings experience rejection throughout their lives. No one has stellar luck and always wins – life doesn't work that way. Recovering from a romantic rejection is excruciatingly painful and can affect a person's self-esteem negatively, often for a long period of time. Working on your self-esteem will enable you to lessen the pain you experience during the healing process and will give you more self-insight so that you can regain your perspective. To begin this process, it's important to recognize when your thinking is distorted.

Distorted thinking causes you to be blind to reality and see yourself and the world in a negative way - you are constantly putting yourself down and not giving yourself credit for your accomplishments. Everything that goes wrong or doesn't work out is all your fault, rather than partially or in some cases mostly due to circumstances beyond your control. You blame yourself for everything because you no longer feel that you are good enough; the breakup pulled the rug out from under you and you're having a hard time standing firmly on the ground. You are your own worst critic and this irrational thinking pattern causes you to undermine yourself. You apply labels to yourself that are inaccurate and harsh. You have an unbalanced view of yourself, the world, and the people around you, including your ex.

One type of distorted thinking that is particularly harmful is making overgeneralizations. For example: Three of your relationships may have failed, so you stop dating because you assume that doing so would be a waste of time. You simply throw up your hands in frustration and give up because you think your relationships are doomed to fail, which becomes a self-fulfilling prophecy. But the reality is totally different – when you sit down and think about everything rationally, you discover that the real reason those three relationships didn't work out was because one woman moved to a different city, another was still involved with an ex-boyfriend, and the last woman you dated had work-related problems, was depressed about her situation, and wasn't open to love, so she shut you out. Many things can happen to cause a relationship to end that aren't remotely close to being 100% your fault. But if you continue telling yourself that your luck is bad you'll never regain the confidence to make an effort to stay in the game and eventually meet the right person. If this is your thinking pattern stop it now. Avoid using sentences like, "Things never work out for me," or, "My relationships always fail." What you're telling yourself is untrue. Instead, replace this thinking pattern with, "I haven't met the right person yet, and I will continue to be open," or, "I know that all women are different people with different personalities and needs. I also know that circumstances beyond my control can positively or negatively affect a relationship." The opposite of this thinking pattern is when you feel like you are a victim and everything that happens to you is the fault of someone else. This mindset is even more detrimental because it keeps you from gaining self-insight, so you repeat behavior that is unhelpful.

Another harmful thinking pattern is when you view the world in extremes. Do you live in a black and white world with no shades of gray? When you categorize everything and everybody sharply in your mind the world becomes a hostile place. An example of this thinking pattern is when you tell yourself: "She was the perfect match for me and now she's gone forever," as if there were no other women in the world. Out of the billions of women on the planet and the millions living close to you, I'm sure that there is someone living nearby who would be a wonderful match for you, although she won't magically come to you, and you'll have to make an effort to find her. But if you think in extremes it will hamper your efforts and hold you back. When you meet other women, you'll eventually find someone interesting who you will want to continue seeing. And you don't know for sure that your ex is gone forever. She might show up on your doorstep one day, something that would be unfortunate, but it could happen. People are complex, and no definitive assumptions should be made about what their actions will be in the future.

Do you apply labels to yourself and others? For example: You've gained a few pounds and your clothing no longer fits. Rather than eat less and exercise more, you label yourself as fat. Because you are applying a negative label to yourself, you lose the confidence to get out of the house, meet women, and date. What you should do is buy yourself a couple of new outfits that fit you well, actively try and meet women, and while dating you can join a gym and get back the body you had before the weight gain.

Negative thinking patterns, although limiting, brings a person relief from their situation in the short-term because fewer risks are taken while they are stagnating. But in the long-term this thinking is extremely damaging. It's easy to blame yourself for everything that goes wrong and not do a thorough analysis of what happened and why. It's also easy to stay attached to the dreamy, unrealistic memory of your ex and not go through the trouble of finding someone new. You will experience some discomfort when you let go of her memory and make a genuine effort to live your life without her. But once the discomfort fades, when you realize that you are the master of your life and not all those negative thoughts holding you back, you will have triumphed.

# Breakup Survival Summaries

- When we're in love we look for our love interest's good qualities and blind ourselves to the bad. Because we do this, after a breakup we are often confused.
- The writing exercise in this chapter will help you to reach an epiphany and you will achieve closure because you'll be able to answer your own questions.
- After doing the exercise, store your lists somewhere you can find them so that you can refer to them in the future if necessary.
- Rid yourself of negative thinking patterns that hold you back in life.

# Chapter Ten

## How to Get Through That One Horrible Day

The process of getting over a breakup is like driving down a road you've never driven before – because it's unfamiliar territory, you don't always see potholes and bumps, so sometimes driving turns rough. But if you accept that you will be hit with situational depression at times the road becomes smoother, and eventually you'll be able to drive on safely without incurring any serious damage. This way of thinking offers a great deal of protection, but even so, along the way, it's not unusual for someone to have one or more difficult days where they are completely stymied and unable to function at all. This day could occur during the first month after the breakup or even farther down the road such as a year later. Getting through this lousy day is much easier if you understand what you're going through, why it's happening, and how to pull through it. There are seven simple steps you can take listed below:

**Step 1:** Find a quiet place so that you can process what's happening. If you're at work, take your lunch break at a park or away from the crowd. If you're at school, you can go to the library and sit in a private study room if one is available.

**Step 2:** Once you're comfortably situated, breathe in through your nose gently and exhale slowly through your mouth. Do this four or five times. This breathing exercise will relax your mind and body immediately.

**Step 3:** Ask yourself what you're feeling and why. When you pinpoint the stressor, you will be less anxious. Defining the problem is the key to feeling better because confusion breeds more anxiety. If you have a pen and paper handy, you can write it down. Or, you can enter the information into the memo section of your cellphone.

**Step 4:** Accept that you're having a bad day and that you know why. Allow your mind to process this information. Everyone has good and bad days. Few people have a string of good days in a row. Most people have crappy days in between good ones, or a string of crappy days and then a string of better ones. That's just how life is and no one, no matter how attractive, successful, or smart can escape that fact.

**Step 5:** Ask yourself if the issue that is causing you stress will matter in a month, a year, or five years from now. Most likely, it won't. But if you think that it might affect you in the long-term, write down why you believe that to be the case and what you can do to turn it around. Take action if you think it's necessary, but do so in a smart way. Oftentimes, problems resolve themselves or become less urgent over time and no action is needed.

**Step 6:** Keep yourself from obsessing about the specific problem or problems that are affecting you during the day by absorbing yourself in your work or studies. When you return home, read over the list you made with all the ideas you had to keep yourself distracted. If there's nothing on it that pops out at you, add some more ideas that you think would work. You might also choose to call a friend so that you don't feel alone.

**Step 7:** Accept the fact that in life things are constantly changing. If you look back in time you'll realize that clothing styles have dramatically changed over the years, as well as music, and culture. Jobs that were once common no longer exist due to technological advances, and new jobs are being created all the time. Tomorrow brings change and things will be different – this is a certainty. Allow yourself to be flexible – similar to how a flower blows in the wind, and remain open-minded about the future. Have confidence that you will get through this difficult time and that things will surely get better. That way you won't get so caught up in the moment.

## Overcoming the Feeling of Being in a Dark Place

The personal story that I will share with you now might seem heavy, but I'm doing it to make an important point – that even when you're hit with one disappointment after another, you can turn things around for the better and enjoy life again.

During the worst breakup of my life with a man that I had been engaged to, I was also given some bad news about my health. Because of the length of time it took me to deal with my illness, I ended up having to leave my job. I was faced with the triple-whammy of losing my partner in life who I loved deeply, having poor health, and losing my livelihood. My occupation was what gave me an identity – a reason to feel proud and accomplished, so losing it and then finding out that I had been replaced was hard. My job had also kept me from thinking about my failed relationship, and since I no longer had a place to go every day, I obsessed about my ex. Going through treatment was difficult, and I had to do it alone. I experienced financial difficulties, could barely cover my bills, and was unable to purchase the home I had saved for years to buy. The world felt unfriendly and I began to feel like an outsider. I would watch people commuting to and from work from my window while I had to stay at home or go to doctor's appointments. On the days I felt slightly better and was able to leave the house, I would walk past restaurants and see couples enjoying a night out together inside – seeing this was a reminder that I had no one. I had the sense that life was something that other people were meant to enjoy, but not me. I felt trapped by the parameters I set for myself – I boxed myself in believing that my present situation would also be my future.

When I was home alone, I would sometimes recall an evening in my early-teens when my friend talked me into going to a nightclub – this memory, that originally had no meaning, ended up meaning everything to me. I had lost track of this friend, but occasionally my sister would mention her when talking about events from our childhood – this is likely what first triggered the memory.

The night my friend and I went to the nightclub we had no ID, and since we were underage, we should not have been allowed inside. Once we entered, I found the environment to be dark and sleazy. The music at that particular club was terrible, so rather than finding it entertaining as I had expected, to me it was deafening – I stuck tissue in my ears so that I could tolerate the noise. The drinks that different men ordered for me made me nauseous, and I sat with people I found scary or by myself for hours while my friend danced. I saw a glowing exit sign in the back, invitingly beckoning me to escape my situation. I sat and stared at it, as if it was the answer to my problem.

When going through my difficulties there were days when that exit sign would stick out in my mind, informing me that I had a way out. I wanted desperately to escape the devastation I felt due to the breakup, my sick body, and the emptiness and continuous struggle that was my life. I would think to myself: Make it stop. I want out. But then my mind would turn to something else that happened on that night, long ago. I realized my mistake in having gone to the club at such a young age. I approached my friend on the dance floor and told her that I was going to leave with or without her. And, to my surprise, she chose to leave with me – through the front door. We ended up going to a restaurant, met up with friends, and had a great time. I often use that analogy when I think about my life and how things ended up unfolding - the choice I made as a teenager was similar to what I did after being dumped by my fiancé and then becoming sick. I was in a nightmare situation and wanted out, but I chose to face the problem and found a solution. When getting over my breakup, because I set the ground rules for my own recovery, I was able to put the relationship behind me. Soon after, my health returned, and things fell into place once again. I had to be patient and work towards pulling myself up by my bootstraps, but I was able to do it. I still have bad days like everyone else, but the good far outweigh the bad. The man that left me came back, but I rejected his advances because although he knew that I was sick, he offered me no help or sympathy, and in my eyes, he bad character. I dated once I got my confidence back and met someone else.

No one is immune from having their partner leave them or getting an unexpected illness. What happened to me can happen to anyone. There are periods in people's lives where they have to fight to keep going, but fighting through difficulties teaches us lessons and widens our minds. During my darkest days I tried to keep myself distracted so that I wouldn't sink further into depression - I decided to create lists which I utilized, and they were effective. I got out of the house as much as I could and met people face-to-face so that I had regular human contact. I learned new skills and started a small business. I exercised when I was able, and it helped pull me out of depression. I did everything I had to do to help myself, and those nuisance gray clouds that seemed to always hang over my head slowly lifted, one cloud at a time. I wouldn't wish what happened to me on anyone else. But I can say from personal experience that you *can* remake your life.

# Breakup Survival Summaries

- Understanding that you'll experience situational depression occasionally while getting over a breakup will help you deal with the bumps on the road on your way to healing.
- Most people will experience at least one extremely difficult day where the stress and anxiety due to the breakup make it hard for them to function. Combined with other difficulties a person might be going through at the same time, the stress a person feels can seem overwhelming.
- You can get through a tough day by following some simple steps that will relax you and help you gain your perspective back.
- Find a quiet place to sit and process what is happening to you. Perform a gentle, slow, breathing exercise to lower the stress you feel immediately.
- Define the problem that's bothering you because once you know exactly what is causing your anxiety, you can face it.
- Accept the fact that you'll have good days and bad days, just like everyone else.
- Ask yourself if the problem causing you stress is a short or long-term issue. If you think that it will affect you in the future, think of a way that you can turn it around. Decide to take intelligent action or allow the problem to resolve itself over time.

- To get through the day so that you can start fresh tomorrow, look over the list you made of ideas you can use to distract yourself. You might also choose to call a friend so that you don't feel alone.
- Change is constant and few things in life remain the same. Tomorrow will be different than today.

# Chapter Eleven

## The Detachment Phase

At some point you will begin to feel a level of detachment from your ex. Once this kicks in, it's important that you allow yourself to follow this state of mind. The beauty of detachment is that it frees you from painful memories. You'll remember what happened, but it will no longer take as big a toll on you emotionally. You'll still think about her, but not every day. And if you begin to obsess about her again you'll have the ability to snap yourself out of it. During this phase of recovery, it's easy to fall into a state of boredom; transitions are often dull. You are used to having intense feelings, but now there is no longer that sense of excitement and curiosity.

The worst thing to do when you're feeling blah is to try and shake things up. Some people are uncomfortable with the feeling of detachment and become disturbed by their lack of emotion; they feel the need to get their heart pounding again. They might contact their ex under the guise of making peace with her, or to suggest a friendship. This is a huge mistake and totally self-defeating. Anyone who does this is putting themselves right back where they started - the first stages of recovery.

The people who recover most quickly from a breakup are those who don't fight detachment. Grudge holders have terrible difficulty getting over a breakup because they take most things personally and don't allow themselves to feel detached. Luckily, most people have the ability to forgive others and themselves and can naturally reach this phase. It's also important when trying to get over a breakup to keep your ego in check because to reach the detachment stage it's necessary to leave your ego at the door. In everyday life a level of narcissism is good. To get ahead in this world you need to believe in yourself and your abilities. But when trying to get over a breakup, instead of helping you it will work against you. If your ego takes a massive hit whenever you experience rejection or fail to reach a goal, you will suffer a lot more than you have to.

## The Awkward In-Between Stage

It's not unusual to have fantasies about making an ex jealous. You might be tempted to post a photo of yourself on social media with your arm around a beautiful woman, hoping your ex will see it. Or, you might dream about bumping into her while on a date with someone else. If something like this were to happen in real life it might give you a momentary ego boost, but in the end, it would be meaningless because the relationship is over anyway. When you begin to feel detached and no longer think about her every day like you did before, you will still have these fantasies at times, but they will go away eventually. Because detachment is a natural process, you might not even realize it's happening. Your life will go on and other interests will develop. One day, she will slip from your mind altogether and you'll be over her.

## Here are a few signs that will tell you when you've gotten over your ex:

1. You no longer fantasize about bumping into her when you're out with a female friend or on a date.
2. You've deleted her from the contacts list in your cellphone so you no longer see her profile photo pop up on the messaging apps you used communicate with her.
3. You're not interested in checking her social media posts to see if she's in a new relationship and what she's been up to.
4. You've stopped hoping that you will someday get back together with her.
5. You're in a new relationship with someone you genuinely care about; you're not on the rebound.
6. When you see your ex out in public with a man, it doesn't devastate you. You don't put much energy into wondering whether he's her colleague, a relative, or date.

7. She might live or work nearby, but you no longer feel her presence as you go about your day.
8. You're driving down the street and see a car whizzing by that looks like your ex's car. You're curious to know if it's her or not, but your curiosity is not strong enough to make you react - your heart doesn't pound faster, and you don't seriously consider driving back to take a look. Instead, you drive on thinking about all the things you have to do that day.

# Breakup Survival
# Summaries

- At some point you will begin to feel detached from your ex. Go with this feeling and don't fight it.
- Being detached might feel boring, but it's a good thing.
- When you've gotten over the breakup, you will no longer wish to get back together with her or fantasize about making her jealous. If you bump into her when she's out with another man it won't devastate you as it would have in the past.
- Eventually, you'll reach a point where you're completely detached, meaning you're over her.

# Chapter Twelve

## Why Breakups Have Become More Traumatic

Although breakups have always been difficult, the usage of messaging apps and social networks, as with most technological advances throughout history, have had unintended consequences. It's so easy for people to communicate quickly using their devices that many have become lazy and rarely make time for face-to-face human interaction, viewing it as an inconvenience that drags them away from work or out of the house. These two modes of communication leave people unable to detect subtle inflections in people's voices, or read their facial expressions and body language making it harder for them to understand one another's true feelings. Messaging apps have effectively taken much of the formality out of dating and promoted the usage of slang, further eroding romance. Video calls are wonderful and allow for better communication than traditional voice calls. However, the easy access of video-mode puts pressure on people to look their best at odd hours of the day when they might be tired or standing in bad lighting.

New techniques have been mastered for dumping people showing a lack of empathy that was rare before the global usage of apps and social networks made it easier for people to flit casually in and out of each other's lives. Being able to communicate with complete strangers on various networks, people have the false sense that they have and endless choice of partners, and many will play games with the people they're dating in order to keep their options permanently open. When these games are played from the outset, deep relationships rarely develop, and breakups are a guessing game. People are left wondering if their relationships were ever real, if they were really dumped, and if their exes will pop up one day unexpectedly and behave as if they were old pals. Cold terms are now commonly used to describe the ambiguity of the situation people find themselves in after being dumped, and what is perpetuated by the "dumper." Some of these terms are: ghosting, zombie-ing, benching, haunting, putting someone on ice, cushioning, and placing someone on simmer. There is a good chance that during your dating life you've experienced one of the infamous techniques described in detail below. The first four are somewhat new while the last three are old-school classics that have been renamed:

- **Ghosting, also known as "vanishing":** When someone wants to instigate a breakup, but can't face the other person they will simply disappear from their life without warning. The person doing the ghosting wants a double-win for themselves – they wish to exit without the sticky inconvenience of a confrontation, while at the same time they want the ability to come back to the person they dumped at a later time if they feel like it because technically, there was no definitive ending. The individual they unexpectedly ceased communicating with is supposed to take the hint that they've been dumped, but be appreciative of the fact that things are being left open.

- **Zombie-ing:** This is a term used to describe the actions of an ex who ghosted you, but pops up months or even years later by sending you a casual chat message, or leaving a comment on your social media page. Essentially, your ex, who you long buried and left in the past suddenly wakes from the dead and begins conversing with you as if you hung out recently and are the best of friends. When this happens it usually means that she has recently come out of a relationship and wants attention from someone she knows once cared for her.

- **Benching:** A commitment-phobic person who doesn't want to feel alone will often date someone they choose to rarely see face-to-face, conducting their relationship mostly on their smartphone. This type of person might be intimate with you a few times in a scattered way and give you all sorts of excuses why they can't see you regularly in person. Yet, at the same time, they shower you with friendly and flattering chat messages so that you don't walk away from them. This sort of behavior seriously messes with the mind of the person on the receiving end of it because at the beginning, they genuinely believe that the bencher is just super-busy. The person who is being benched wants a relationship with the bencher, but since it never really happens they are often strung along for months or years, hoping for something that never truly materializes. If, in the future, you see that your relationship is taking place mostly online, know that you are being benched or otherwise being held at arm's length for a reason that only the bencher knows.

- **Haunting:** This occurs after a breakup when the person who was dumped begins noticing comments on their social media page from their ex. The haunter is attempting to reconnect casually but not trying to get back together because if she wanted to do that she would call or send a chat message, both higher levels of communication. She might be seeking attention, hoping for a response that will stroke her ego. Or, she feels guilty about the breakup and wants her ex to respond in a mild or friendly way so that she doesn't feel so bad about how she treated him. The kindest thing to do would be to leave the man she dumped alone, but she lacks empathy and is too selfish to realize this.

- **Putting someone on ice:** This is the act of starting a relationship with someone, and then backing away so that a real commitment is never made. But no breakup is instigated, and contact is still made occasionally, usually after weeks or months have gone by, giving the person on the receiving end the sensation that they are being stored for later use. People who put others on ice are attempting to keep their options open while dating, or they might not know exactly what they are looking for in a partner. They become romantically involved with a man because they don't want to be alone, or they are dating more than one person and putting them all in the freezer when it suits them. They find the man they are placing on ice attractive or they wouldn't have started dating him in the first place, but they aren't absolutely certain that he is the one for them. They believe that when they find the right person they will know it, but this turns out not to be the case in the long run and they often regret putting a man on ice who they later believe was "the one."

- **Cushioning:** This phenomenon occurs when someone who is in a relationship that is unsatisfying begins to date before they are emotionally or financially ready to leave their partner. They date so that they will have other people on standby should they have the guts one day to exit their situation. But feeling comfortable, and concerned about the fallout if they actually left, they end up wasting the time of the men they date who believe that they are single or in the process of ending a difficult relationship. The men get the sense that they've been put on ice but rarely realize that they are being used as cushions.

- **Placing someone on simmer:** This is an attempt at a slow breakup. The special person in your life communicates with you less and less over time, similar to a downward sliding scale, hoping that you will become frustrated and exit the situation so that they don't have to feel guilty about dumping you. They start the process by calling and making plans with you less and less over several weeks or months, like air slowly being let out of a balloon. Eventually, you notice that all the recent plans you made as a couple were cancelled and realize that you are supposed to simply accept the fact that you've been dumped.

Eventually, people who play games and break up with others in the ways discussed above end up experiencing the same thing themselves and are hurt too - this is the world they live in. This vicious cycle of insensitivity erodes trust and also makes it harder to rekindle relationships because people become afraid to let their guard down from the get-go.

When someone rejects another person romantically, they are showing them kindness and respect by letting them down once, and being direct about it. Popping in and out of someone's life is a cruel tease and should never be done – it displays the worst sort of insensitivity. People often say that in love there are no rules, but there are – these are the rules you set for yourself. It might appear to you that everyone is behaving in a similar way and that you have to put up with it because unless you do, you will be alone. But guess what – when you're with someone who plays mind-games, you are alone anyway. It's like having an imaginary friend instead of a lover. In the future, if you begin to feel that a woman you're involved with is playing games with you, or you sense that she's ambivalent, you can simply ask her, "Would you like to remain in this relationship with me, or do you want out?" By saying this you're letting her know that you are aware of her ambivalence and want her to make a decision so that she doesn't drag you along an empty highway for months or years. This allows you to clear the path for someone who is sure about you and who you can develop a tangible connection with. To protect yourself from all the soul-draining nonsense, communicate with the next woman you become involved with mainly in person and limit the time you spend chatting with her using your phone.

# Breakup Survival Summaries

- One of the unintended consequences of smartphone usage is that these devices have made the quality of human interaction much poorer than it was before. Hiding behind messaging apps and conversing on platforms, people have become desensitized to one another's feelings and needs. For this same reason, breakups have become crueler and uglier.
- People fade in and out of each other's lives creating an ambiguous environment that leaves people wondering if their relationships are stable.
- People now break up with each other in ways that they would have been chastised for in the recent past. But they get away with it because it appears that everyone else is doing the same thing. There is no reasonable excuse for showing a lack of sensitivity, but unfortunately, this behavior is now more accepted than it was in the past by society.
- Communicate less on your phone and more in person with the next woman you become involved with so that you can develop something real and meaningful.

# Chapter Thirteen

## The Complexities of Getting Back Together with an Ex and Why It Rarely Works Out

After a breakup, no matter how hard you try to erase your ex from your memory, she will remain in the forefront of your mind for several weeks or months. But as time goes by, she will slip slowly backward, little by little, until her memory reaches the back corners of your mind, although some trace of her will likely always remain. As you go about your life, memories will be triggered by events happening or by your surroundings. You might decide to paint your bedroom a new color, and even though you think that a certain shade of blue would look best, you will avoid using it because it was your ex's favorite color. Or, your friends will suggest taking a trip to Las Vegas, but you will tell them that you are unable to join them, not because you're busy, but because you were married in that city and just being there might depress you. This sort of visceral reaction could happen even twenty years after your divorce. However, memories that pop up every few years don't mean that you want to get back together with your ex, or that you have feelings of love or hatred towards her that you've carried for a long time. It simply means that she occupies some tiny territory in your head. Most people, as they grow older, become accustomed to this and accept it as a part of life. But not everyone is the same, and although rare, sometimes a person will reach out to an ex because they want to rekindle an old flame or simply want to be friends. But whatever their desired outcome, rarely do things turn out as they imagined.

## What makes a person consider getting back together with their ex?

- After a failed relationship, a person might reflect on what occurred that caused their breakup and view their ex in a more positive light. They might come to the conclusion that what they walked away from was worth fighting for. If they choose to contact their ex and that individual still has feelings for them too, they might be able to get back together.
- After having been in other relationships, a person might reminisce about a past relationship. If the memory of a first love or a romantic interest from years ago still haunts them, they might reach out to that person. If

their past love is available and interested,
it's possible that something can develop.

- When someone is in an unfulfilling relationship, they might come to the realization that an earlier relationship was far better, and regret having given up on it. They might contact their ex and request a second chance. This situation can be terribly messy, and a lot of upheaval can occur because one or both people involved might be married.

- Sometimes a memory is triggered in someone's mind that they can't shake. They get a surge of feeling and want to meet up with their ex to relive memories that over the years became important to them.

- Many people are walking around still thinking about "The one that got away." They continue to dream about an ex who they felt was a quality person and had desirable attributes. They regret not having appreciated this person's wonderful qualities when they were in the relationship and might decide to contact them, hoping for another chance.

- Someone who directed most of their energy towards their career or educational goals might regret not taking a past relationship seriously; they may have had a casual relationship with someone they cared for but chose not to take it a step further. Once they've reached their goals and their mind becomes clearer, they begin to think about that person and reach out to them.

# Why are most couples unable to reconcile?

- If one person wishes to reconcile with a past love, but their love interest is in a happy relationship, reconciliation is unlikely to occur. Both people must want to get back together at the same time.
- When someone tries to get their ex back using aggressive tactics, their ex might switch off emotionally, shutting them out completely. Making public scenes, being overly dramatic, stalking, contacting them several times a week, or messaging them non-stop will make it less likely that the relationship will ever be rekindled because the person on the receiving end will want to escape the stress of it all.
- After a breakup, if one person contacts the other on a regular basis under the guise of friendship, it gives their ex no room to realize their loss.
- Some people take the attitude of: What's done is done. They look forward, never backward, and cannot be convinced to try again.
- If one person behaves in a hot and cold manner during a relationship, meaning that they get together with their partner in fits and starts, it can create a situation where their partner literally doesn't know if they are even *in* a relationship. The uncertainty of their situation eventually causes them to look elsewhere for attention and affection. By the time the person who is hot and cold realizes that their relationship has fizzled, their love interest is

with someone new and cannot be convinced to return to an unstable situation.

- When attraction is strong, and a great deal of passion exists between two people, but they are not connected in any other way, if their relationship ends it is unlikely that it can be revived. Physical attraction is fantastic, but it doesn't equal something lasting, and it can't be the only basis for a relationship. There also needs to be trust, respect, and the two people should have mutual interests.
- Lifestyle issues and personal preferences about where to live and whether to have children are important for every couple to discuss. Sometimes, two people are in love but desire totally different things in life. This means that if they break up, getting back together will not be plausible.
- If one person cheated and that's why the relationship ended - because of a lack of trust - it can be incredibly difficult to build that trust again.
- One bad memory can remain in a person's head for a lifetime. Although people tend to remember the good times and try to forget the bad, if an ex contacts them out of the blue they might weigh the good against the bad. If their ex comes up short on what they view as the good side, they will avoid that person.
- If there was verbal abuse, or worse, one person became violent at some point during the relationship the chance that it can be rekindled are slim, understandably. No one should ever

101

consider getting back together with someone who was abusive towards them.

Couples that get back together, separate, and then get back together again are doing what I call "ping-ponging." This pattern can occur for several reasons: There might be a highly charged chemistry between two people, and although they don't get along outside of the bedroom and are aware on some level that they're wasting each other's time, they don't have the strength to walk away completely. It might be that neither person can find a new partner after their breakup who meets their needs, so they get back together with their ex, but then realize for the umpteenth time that it was a mistake. When two people engage in ping-ponging, the drama it creates can throw their lives off course, and even damage their health and ability to earn a living. If a couple tries once and fails, trying another time is not a far-fetched idea if both are willing to make concessions. But getting back together several times often wastes precious time and leads to sheer misery for the couple themselves and everyone around them, including their friends and family who will eventually say to them while rolling their eyes, "Oh, no. Not her again!"

# Breakup Survival Summaries

- Sometimes a person will reminisce about a past relationship and contact their ex. When they do, usually the timing is off by months or years and the relationship can't be revived due to a variety of reasons.
- Relationships can rarely be rekindled because both people must want to get back together at the exact same time for this to occur. Usually, after some time has passed, at least one person will have begun a relationship with someone new, or they will decide that they don't want to try a second time with their ex.
- It's not unheard of for couples to get back together, but both people must be willing to make concessions for it to work. Not everyone has the diplomatic skills to pull this off.
- Getting back together with an ex and then breaking up again several times eventually becomes a foolish endeavor.

# Chapter Fourteen

## Your Ex Resurfaces

### The Guessing Game

Most women, when they want to speak with an ex-boyfriend, will approach him in a subtle way at first in an attempt to get a response. If the man hasn't changed his phone number, a woman might use a messaging app to send him a simple chat message such as, "Hi, how are you?" If she doesn't get the response she wants or is ignored, a phone call is usually the next step. When an ex contacts you, the conversation is unlikely to go smoothly and will be choppy at best.

If your ex decides to contact you, it might play out like this: You're on your way home from work and your cellphone rings – you answer, and realize it's her. You noticed that she left a friendly comment on your social media page three days earlier, but you didn't know how to respond to it because you weren't sure what it meant, so you did nothing. You politely say hello and there is a long pause as you wait for her to speak. Finally, she asks you what you've been up to lately, and you tell her basic details about your life, but you remain silent afterwards, waiting for her to explain why she called. Rather than volunteer this information, she talks about her job, and then rambles off some mundane facts about your mutual acquaintances. As quickly and unexpectedly as she called, she tells you that she should go, indicating that it's now your turn to open up. There is another long pause as she waits for you to say something, but you're not exactly sure what she wants to hear. Sounding disappointed, she makes a few quick remarks, says goodbye, and then hangs up. After this brief interaction, you are either left feeling elated because she's just proven that you're still on her mind, or irritated because the surprise of her call caused you further confusion and anxiety. Calls like this from an ex are not uncommon. Maybe she'll call again and attempt to reconcile. Or, she might choose to call the one time and never call again. It's likely she will view calling you as throwing the ball in your court; she will wait for you to make the next move. Breakups are rarely clean events where both people write each other off and move on, or get back together and live happily ever after. There are moments when people miss their ex and moments when they're glad that the relationship ended.

It's a good idea to have a plan in case she calls. If she were to phone you at a time when you were able to speak freely, you could take the initiative and tell her about any regrets you have and how you've been feeling. Doing so might not have its intended effect; she might not respond the way you would like her to. However, expressing yourself is helpful when trying to achieve closure if you're lucky enough to have the opportunity. If she suggests getting back together, you should ask her why in a diplomatic way. Also, ask her what would be different this time.

## Know What's in Your Best Interest

If you and your ex have been apart for at least a few weeks, you should be able to put on your rational thinking cap. In all likelihood, you will have a visceral response to the sound of her voice. If it causes you to become irritated, you won't need to do any soul-searching - you can be confident that you don't want to have contact with her again. If you have a sentimental response or you want her back strongly, you should take some time to check your emotions. The best way to do this is to refer to your four lists (the exercise from **Chapter Nine**). Read them over carefully and let the words sink in. After reading your lists, set them aside and do some thinking.

How do you feel about her now? Do you know in your heart that if you were to give the relationship a second chance, you would only end up right back where you are now – getting over another breakup with her? If you broke up because she cheated on you, can you get past it? And, do you trust her not to do it again? If she broke up with you by vanishing unexpectedly, isn't it likely that she would repeat that behavior?

# Three Things to Consider:

1. You've already been in a relationship with this person and it ended. If you were to estimate a chance of the relationship succeeding a second time around, what percentage would you assign to that? Is it 50%? Or, is it as low as 20%? Assign a percentage that sounds right to you. By making this judgment you're not being an optimist or pessimist. You're being a realist. If you think that there would be slim chance that the relationship would survive, why try again?

2. When you're in a relationship, you are off the market. If you see no long-term, tangible future with your ex, why start seeing her again and close the door on dating other women?

3. Your time is precious. Don't waste it with someone who isn't the right person for you. If the two of you aren't on the same page, and are constantly arguing and having more difficulties than you can handle, it's not a satisfying relationship. You can find someone else and have a relationship that adds quality to your life instead of draining your energy and making you miserable.

If your ex is calling you and you're flirting with the idea of seeing her again, consider everything that happened in the past, and make the assumption that if you were to get back together with her you would be living with similar, if not the exact same conditions.

# Breakup Survival
# Summaries

- Being contacted by an ex out of the blue is not uncommon. Sometimes it means something, and other times it holds no real significance.
- If her call makes you angry and anxious, you will know that no matter how she feels, you don't want to see her again. If her call makes you want her back, take the time to do a reality check.
- Pull out your four lists from **Chapter Nine** and read them over carefully.
- If you're considering seeing her again, know that if you were to get back together with her, you would most likely be living with the same conditions as before the breakup.
- You have other options in life including the chance to date other women. Getting back together with your ex will get in the way of those opportunities.

# Chapter Fifteen

## Four Breakup Stories

John, Paul, Steve, and Aiden are four men who experienced traumatic breakups. John's girlfriend kept him in the dark about what was going on at her workplace. Paul's girlfriend had a past experience that affected her relationship with him. Steve found out that his girlfriend had made future plans that didn't involve him. And Aiden, who had recently proposed to the woman he loved, got an unpleasant surprise. All four men deal with the end of their relationships in very different ways.

### John's Breakup

John, a thirty-two-year-old software engineer had met Patricia, a twenty-seven-year-old critical care nurse, at a restaurant they both frequented. John saw her there several times before mustering up the courage to invite her to his table to join him for lunch. He slowly courted her and eventually they dated each other exclusively. They had been together for over a year, and their relationship was going strong. Since Patricia and John both normally worked an average of fifty hours per week, the only time they had to spend together was on weekends. In the bedroom, there was an intense chemistry between them, and John felt that Patricia was all he ever wanted or needed. Patricia, a brunette with aqua eyes and small, doll-like facial features, had an hourglass figure. She purposefully played down her looks at work, wearing a low ponytail, minimal makeup, and a drab, loose-fitting mint-green uniform. But outside of her workplace she had her own distinct style – she would often wear fashionable dresses, or jeans and colorful blouses that flattered her complexion, and called attention to the brightness of her eyes. John sometimes wondered why Patricia had never dated any of the doctors or technicians she'd worked with at the hospital, prior to meeting him. At the beginning of their relationship, he'd asked her about this, and Patricia had responded by telling him that during college she had worked at a restaurant and dated someone she met on the job - the relationship ended badly, and she was fired. Because of that experience, she had decided to never again put herself in that situation.

John was thinking about asking Patricia to move in with him, hoping that they would marry soon after, when unexpectedly, he was given a new work assignment. For several weeks he would have to travel back and forth from the company's head office in Austin, Texas. This meant that he wouldn't be able to spend every weekend with Patricia like he had done for most of their relationship. He had no choice but to accept the assignment because it was a project that he was leading. When John called Patricia at work to inform her, she sounded disappointed but was supportive. She wished him luck and asked him to send her a chat message from his cellphone before getting on the plane, which he did.

As the weeks passed, John became more involved with the project than he had anticipated. After four months of traveling back and forth and missing every weekend but one with Patricia, he began noticing a change in how she related to him. In person, she acted the same. The change was only evident when he called her. She would usually ring him back during her work breaks if he phoned her during the day, and she would answer his calls at night. But she didn't sound like her usual self and she refused to put any of their calls on video-mode so that they could speak face-to-face. Her excuses were always the same – the lighting was bad, or she wasn't wearing makeup and felt self-conscious. John understood that she didn't like to be on camera, but she refused to let him see her even once. He couldn't figure out what the problem was, and wondered why she seemed formal and distant. Other than phone conversations, she sent him chat messages about political troubles she was having at work. These messages always ended with an "xox" or a heart emoji. However, she had stopped referring to him as "sweetheart." Even though there was obviously something wrong, he figured that maybe he was over-thinking things and decided not to make a big deal out of it. He would ask her why she was acting cooler towards him the next time he spoke with her.

Finally, John returned to his normal schedule and was told by his office that he would remain in San Francisco for the rest of the year. He called Patricia the minute he knew that he would be free over the weekend to let her know the good news. Patricia, who was on her lunch break, answered the call.

"Hi, honey. I'm not going to be traveling anymore. What do you want to do this weekend?" John asked.

John once again noticed the distant tone in Patricia's voice when she said, "I don't know. Let me think about it. I've got to get back to work now."

Never one to keep his opinions to himself for long, John said, "Okay, that's fine. I don't want to bother you. But, you seem distant. Is it work or me?"

Patricia, taken off-guard, paused before saying, "I don't have the time to get into it now. I'll call you tonight."

That evening, Patricia phoned John and asked him if they could skip their upcoming weekend together. When he asked her why, she told him that she needed to make more money and would have to start working every other Saturday.

"Patricia, you're going to exhaust yourself. I think you should lessen your hours, not add more."

"It's complicated," Patricia said. "I need to work more hours for now. But, you're right. I am a bit tired."

John decided not to ask Patricia any further questions and ended the conversation on a pleasant note. "If you're comfortable with adding more hours to your schedule, I support your decision," he said.

**When Friday evening rolled around,** John received a call from Chris and Margot, a couple that he and

Patricia often double-dated with. Chris invited John to have dinner with them the next evening without inquiring about Patricia. Finding this odd, John asked him to put Margot on the phone.

"Hi, John. Did you want me to try and get reservations for that French restaurant you mentioned a few weeks ago?" she asked.

"The reservation will have to be for three not four. Patricia is working."

"I figured that," Margot said.

"Did you talk to her?"

"Not recently, I just figured, that's all," Margot replied. "So, you want me to go ahead with reserving a table?"

"Sure, that would be fine," John responded. He didn't want to be by himself and he also wanted to share his concerns about Patricia with mutual friends. Maybe Margot would know about Patricia's money problems, or whatever else was going on with her that she didn't seem to want to discuss with him.

At 8 p.m. on Saturday night, Chris sent a message to John's cellphone informing him that he and Margot were waiting outside. John grabbed his wallet and jacket, and then hopped into the back of their car. The ride to the restaurant was quieter than usual. Chris and Margot tended to have minor spats, oftentimes in front of other people. But they were strangely nice to each other that evening.

When they arrived at the restaurant it was packed with people and they had to shout to speak with one another while waiting to be seated. Twenty minutes later, they were escorted to their table and began pouring over the menu. It was longer than they had expected and written mostly in French. Struggling with his French pronunciation, John asked Margot to order for him.

The evening took its usual course and Chris and Margot began to argue by the time dessert arrived. John escaped into his own private thoughts, hoping they would resolve whatever issue they were unable to agree upon. He began to daydream about what the sourdough bread would taste like if he were at a restaurant in Paris, when Margot snapped her fingers in front of him. "Anyone home?" she asked.

"I'm sorry, what were saying?"

"I was just pointing out that attractive brunette standing at the bar. Do you see her?" she said, gesturing towards the bar area.

John turned around, torquing his body into an uncomfortable position to see what was going on behind him. He saw the woman she was talking about. She was quite beautiful and looked like Patricia, only younger. "Yes, very pretty."

"She doesn't appear to be on a date. She came in with that blonde girl standing next to her," Margot said. "She probably comes here a lot."

"It seems to be a popular place," John replied.

"There are loads of gorgeous women that come in here," Chris said, nodding.

John suddenly got the uncomfortable feeling that his friends were trying to tell him something. He wondered why they would disrespect Patricia in such a way. True to form, John asked, "You two have decided that I can somehow do better than Patricia?"

"We didn't say that," Margot responded, sarcastically. "We don't think that *you* think that way. It's *her* we have our doubts about."

114

John's head was spinning. He didn't understand why Margot was suddenly picking on Patricia. They had been double dating for months, and Margot and Patricia seemed to have gotten along well. At least, Patricia hadn't mentioned anything to him. Chris chimed in, "We love Patricia. She's great. Let's talk about something else."

When John got home it was after midnight. He was so bothered by the conversation at dinner that he called Patricia, even though he knew she would be annoyed by a call so late. To his surprise, she answered immediately. "John? What's going on?" she asked, wide awake and curious.

"I went out with Chris and Margot tonight. I just got home," he said. "Is there a problem between you and Margot? She's acting strangely. Did you two have a falling out?"

Patricia paused before saying, "No. We aren't really close friends. I mean, at least I consider her more of an acquaintance."

"Yes, I understand, but did something happen?"

"She came to have lunch with me at the hospital a couple of weeks ago. I was with a friend and she saw us together at the cafeteria. She came too early."

"What friend?"

"John, I think that I should be honest with you. There was someone I once dated who is now working at the hospital. He's an orthopedist. Margot came to her own conclusions when she saw us sitting together, having coffee. He and I have gone out a few times."

John was taken aback. "What do you mean by *gone out?*"

"I mean we've gone to lunch and dinner together. I was always with you on weekends, so I told him that I

115

was busy. But you ended up spending a lot of time in Austin. So, I started seeing him."

"You're seeing this doctor now? You're *dating* him?" John asked, astonished.

"Yes...I mean...I suppose you could look at it that way," Patricia answered, quietly.

"Are you going to continue with this? You're going to date both of us? No wonder you're so tired," John said, raising his voice.

"Don't shout at me. I was confused. Now, I'm more confused. But I don't appreciate being yelled at," Patricia said.

"I'm not yelling at you. I'm just shocked. I had no idea. I didn't see this coming. How did you expect me to react?"

"You're shouting at me," she said. "I'm hanging up."

John stood as still as a statue - he couldn't believe what he had just heard. He then started pacing the floor of his bedroom, trying to think through everything that had occurred. Still holding his cellphone, his hand began shaking. He stopped pacing when he came to an important conclusion, and sat down on the corner of his bed. He realized that simply by raising his voice he had given Patricia the out she needed. He hadn't actually yelled at her, and under the circumstances, he had handled the situation with tact. She had pretended he'd shouted and reacted in an aggressive manner, so that she could feel less guilty about ditching him for the doctor.


John awoke the next morning, depressed and still reeling from his conversation with Patricia. He tried to work through it by thinking out loud. "She indicated that the orthopedist had been asking her out regularly, meaning that he was chasing her, not the other way around. Also, if she liked him so much, why didn't she break up with me? Obviously, she has feelings for me. Maybe she intended to see us both until she made up her mind about which one of us she wanted to be with. But then, why did she behave in a dismissive way over the phone? Most likely, because she got caught and had to make a quick decision."

John's thoughts crushed him inside, causing him to feel so depressed that he couldn't get out of bed for hours. He lay there rationalizing, trying to cope with the unexpected situation he found himself in. At the same time, he wanted to remain optimistic - there was still a chance that he could save his relationship. It was possible that Patricia hadn't been intimate with the doctor. Flirting and going to dinner did not equal intimacy. However, she did tell him that she'd never dated anyone at work. Even though it was likely that she and the doctor never worked directly together, Patricia working in critical care and the doctor, in orthopedics, she still had lied to him.

John had loads of work to do during the week, so he tried his best to put the situation with Patricia out of his mind. But by Wednesday, he couldn't stop thinking about it and called her on her cellphone. When she didn't answer, he sent her a chat message: *I'm sorry I became upset the last time we spoke. I don't want to blame you. It's an occupational hazard, you being an attractive nurse working at a large hospital. Someone is bound to hit on you, and I was away most of the time. We can work this out. Please give me a call.*

117

After waiting anxiously for days and getting no response, John concluded that Patricia either didn't want to answer him in a chat message, or that she would never respond. John checked his office email religiously under normal circumstances, but he began checking it more often, hoping that she might reach out to him. After two weeks, he finally noticed an email from her in his inbox. His heart pounded quickly in his chest as he opened it. She wrote: *John, you had every reason to be angry. I apologize for letting you down. In all honesty, I am involved with Thomas. I care for you, but I'm with him now. I'm very sorry and I wish you well.*

Patricia's polite rejection meant that there was no hope of reconciliation. Devastated once more, John told his colleagues that he wasn't feeling well and went home early.

**Heartbroken and disappointed,** John threw himself into his work, using it as an escape. A group of old friends from his college days who knew about the breakup began calling him in an attempt to get him to go out with them, but John had no interest in socializing and told them repeatedly that he was busy. He found little joy in anything other than the occasional interesting project he was given at work. Although his job was stressful, he was grateful that he had a place to go every day, allowing him to keep his mind from wandering and thinking about Patricia. He ignored Chris and Margot's calls, feeling that if they had known something they should have been honest with him, or at least prepared him emotionally for the massive letdown they knew was coming his way. Maybe if he had known the whole story, he could have handled the situation better, he told himself. He might have been able to contain his emotions and strategize so that he could woo Patricia back. On other days he felt that Chris and Margot were innocents, only their penchant for gossip annoyed him.

Nearly a month went by before John's close friend, Mark dropped by unexpectedly on a Saturday afternoon, stating that he was concerned about his well-being. John, who was watching a boring movie and drinking a brand of beer he didn't particularly care for invited Mark in. After sitting next to him on the sofa in an uncomfortable silence, Mark decided to try and snap his friend out of his doldrums. "You can't sit here like this forever. Life goes on. Her life is going on, but yours has come to a full-stop. That's not right. All you do is work, come home, and sit by yourself. You need to at least get out of the house."

John was fully aware that his mood was consistently sour. He missed Patricia badly and had tried everything to get her to speak with him. He had left her messages on social media, emailed her, called her, and had lost count of how many times he'd messaged her on her phone, but she continued to ignore him. She had left behind a white chemise, and her toothbrush was still sitting in a cup in the bathroom. John knew that he should throw these things out, but in the back of his mind he hoped desperately that she would come back to him. If she did, he would show her that he hadn't touched her things and that everything remained the same.

After a great deal of coaxing, Mark was able to get John to walk to a restaurant two blocks from his house. The fresh cool air jolted John back to life as he stepped out the door. He looked around at all the cars parked on his street, some of them with tickets on their windshields, and was suddenly aware that people were going about their everyday lives – all except for him. When they reached the Italian restaurant, the liveliness of the crowd was in stark contrast to his quiet moping at home. Once they sat down at a booth, they ordered calzones and two beers. But when the food arrived, John, having little appetite, only took a couple of bites. "You've got to start eating. You're looking thin," Mark said.

John, feeling fortunate to have a friend as good as Mark, began cutting into his calzone and took decent sized bites. Once he started eating, he began to perk up enough that he felt he could verbalize what he was going through. Mark listened patiently to John's confused story and tried to lift his spirits. When they finished lunch, and returned to John's home, Mark walked into the bathroom and tossed Patricia's toothbrush in the trash. Afterwards, he walked into the bedroom, found Patricia's chemise, and made a deal with John. "I'll be taking this with me. If she comes back, I'll give it back to you. I doubt that will happen, so let me know when you want me to throw it out, and I will."

The second month after the breakup was the hardest for John. He would sit for hours looking at a collection of photos he had taken of Patricia that he'd saved on his phone. The pictures gave him the sense that a part of her was still with him, even though he knew that wasn't the case in reality. Mark continued to call him regularly, and when John chose to ignore him, he would sometimes drop by his house and force him to go out.

Another month passed before John's dark mood began to lift. He was given a project at work that he was excited about, and it consumed most of his time. He enjoyed it so much that he began staying late at the office, coming up with cutting edge ideas. This led to some great opportunities for him and his company. Within a few months, John was on a winning streak. People in his field began to recognize him and his name started to carry weight. Another company approached him, attempting to steal him away from their main competitor. When his company found out, they immediately began paying him more and offered him a better position.

John continued to put all his efforts into his work, but when the attention started to wane he began to feel lonely, and once again, felt the sting of losing Patricia. He wondered if she was still dating the doctor and began obsessing about her. Late one evening, determined to get her back, he picked up the phone to call her. But at that moment, Mark called and invited him to watch the NBA Playoffs at a mutual friend's house that upcoming Saturday. John was agitated and tried to get off the phone with him in a polite way, but Mark didn't catch the hint and continued to talk. Hoping to finally get him off the phone, John gave him his word that he would go. But by the time their conversation ended, it was after 1 a.m. Irritated with his friend, and knowing that Patricia was unlikely to answer her phone at that hour, he decided against calling her.

* * *

When John arrived at the get-together, he immediately noticed that the ratio was out of balance - there were six women and nearly twenty men. This was an irrelevant fact to John, until one of the women caught his eye – a young brunette. She sat on a cushioned ivory armchair close to the television, watching the game and endlessly eating potato chips from a glass bowl in her lap. John found her attractive in her tight t-shirt and baggy sweatpants. Her high-ponytail hung lazily to the side of her head, and she hardly wore any makeup. But in John's opinion, she didn't need any. Taking a seat in the chair next to her, he chatted with her during the commercials about sports and asked her what team she wanted to win. She leaned towards him, pointed to some barely visible writing across her chest, and told him, "Read my shirt."

As John was getting ready to leave that evening he grabbed his coat and approached Sam, the host of the party, to ask him about the woman in the sweatpants. Sam was in the garage where he kept a second refrigerator. After pulling out several bottles of cold beer, he closed the refrigerator door and spoke with John. "That's Kate, my sister's friend. She and my sister are staying with me for a few days until they move into a place together. They're going to be roommates."

"How old do you think she is?" asked John, standing back, allowing Sam to pass him.

"She's exactly the same age as my sister - twenty-six," Sam said, walking up the steps leading back into the house.

"Is Sarah really twenty-six already? I can't believe it."

Sam turned and looked at John as if he had just said something ridiculous. "Time moves forward," he said.

A week after the party, John was jogging around a park near his home when his cellphone in his sweatshirt pocket rang. He fumbled around looking for it, and then stopped to see who was calling. Seeing Sam's name pop up, he immediately answered, but to his surprise a woman's voice was on the other end.

"John? Hey, it's Kate. Remember me from last week?"

John was pleasantly surprised. "Yes, of course. How are you?" he said, catching his breath.

"Are you busy today?"

"Not particularly. I'm jogging now, but I'll be heading home soon."

"Sarah and I need some extra help moving into our apartment. Sam said to call you to see if you were free. He's spending the day helping us. We're at his place now."

John knew that Sam would have never suggested anything of the sort. He and Sam had been roommates in college. Sam knew that he was lazy and not keen on lifting furniture. "Sam knows me well. Of course, I'd be glad to help. I can get there in an hour. Is that okay?"

"Sure, we'll be here. See you then," said Kate, ending the call.

John spent the day helping Kate and Sarah move into their new apartment. Sam was shocked by John's can-do attitude about lifting and carrying boxes. John's interest in Kate gave him a strong incentive. Later that evening they all went to dinner and Kate was forthright about her romantic interest in John. She admitted to him that Sam had mentioned his concerns about asking him to help. She also told him that he looked a lot like an actor who she had always found attractive. John had no idea who she was talking about, but accepted the compliment.

John and Kate began dating, but spending time alone with each other was a problem. John couldn't invite Kate to his place for weeks because his two nieces were visiting from New York, scouting out colleges and spending time with family. He knew that if he introduced her to them that the whole family would become curious and pester him about the new woman in his life. He didn't need the stress, and he didn't want to put Kate through a family dinner so early in their relationship. They couldn't spend much time at Kate's apartment either because the place she shared with Sarah was small and Sarah's boyfriend was there nearly every day. They finally became intimate when they took a trip together to Napa Valley. They had planned on a three-day trip, but stayed an extra day because they enjoyed their time together and didn't want it to end.

When their trip was over, and John reached home after dropping off Kate, he checked his cellphone and saw a chat message from Patricia. In it, she asked him how he was and if he wanted to meet up. Surprised, his first inclination was to respond that he was fine and ask her if she wanted to meet up somewhere. But he decided to unpack from the trip instead, and check emails from the office. His mind on other things, he forgot to respond that night and went to sleep.

A week passed, and John decided to ignore Patricia's message. He still had feelings for her, but his mind was geared towards his relationship with Kate. He was falling in love with her and didn't have the desire to reconnect with Patricia.

Two years later, John and Kate are still seeing each other. Kate has dropped hints about getting married, and John respects the fact that she wants something permanent. He's planning to propose to her on their next trip out of town together.


## Paul's Breakup

Paul, a successful forty-year-old, was the owner of a construction company. His main focus was residential, and he proudly built high quality homes. During one of his busiest years he met Gabriella, a thirty-seven-year-old divorced mother of two, and began a relationship with her. Gabriella also owned her own business - a clothing boutique for women.

Paul had been married in his early twenties, but it quickly ended, and he had no children. He had great admiration for Gabriella; he was impressed that she was able to raise two children, a six-year-old boy, and an eight-year-old girl, all by herself. When Gabriella first met Paul, she explained that she had gotten married at the age of twenty-seven and was happy for the first few years. But her husband began cheating on her when she was pregnant with their second child which caused problems in their marriage. She forgave him, hoping that he would put the welfare of his family first. However, he cheated again, and it became a pattern. She told Paul that she'd filed for divorce when her son turned four. Paul couldn't fathom why anyone would cheat on a beautiful and kind person like Gabriella. And he felt badly that the children didn't have a father at home.

Gabriella, a petite, classy, well-dressed woman, had a slim figure and ample bustline. She was a member of the gym across the street from her boutique and kept herself in great shape. A platinum blonde with straight hair that reached her shoulders, and wispy bangs that fell just above her dark eyes, she had a warmth about her. Gabriella was also amazingly intelligent; she had an innate ability to discuss almost any subject with ease. Paul was in love with her, and looked forward to seeing her on average, three times a week. She had introduced Paul to her children, but also distanced them from him. She explained that if their relationship reached a point where they agreed to marry, then of course, they would be a family. But she felt that a serious commitment such as marriage needed to be taken slowly, and Paul agreed. Gabriella was also guarded and protective of her feelings. Paul felt that she had difficulty trusting men because of what had happened during her marriage.

Paul had been dating Gabriella for just over two years when suddenly, the business climate began to change. People were no longer putting deposits down on properties, and many that did, asked for it back stating that they could no longer afford to buy. Paul had seen the tide changing, but was surprised by the extent of the downturn and how quickly it occurred. It got so bad that he had to cancel all projects except for one that he was determined to finish. He began lowering prices and adding upgrades so that people would continue to buy and move into their newly built homes. Even with those incentives, he realized huge losses, and within a few months, he, as well as many of his competitors were nearly bankrupt. Paul had experienced ups and downs in business before. He had owned two businesses that failed in the past, but nothing even remotely like this.

As he tried to pull himself out of his financial mess, Paul began calling Gabriella less and less, and stopped dropping by her boutique to take her to out to dinner on her slow nights. He was in a horrible state of mind and his confidence was at an all-time low. Paul felt like he had gone from hero to zero. He had seen himself in a different light before - only a few months ago, if he and Gabriella had decided to marry, he would have been able to support her and her children. But in his present financial position he felt that he would only be a burden.

In an attempt to lift his spirits, Paul began hanging out at a sports bar with friends he hadn't seen in months because he had been busy working and spending all of his free time with Gabriella. Late on a Wednesday night, he and his friends, Mike and Kevin, were playing pool in the back of the bar when three women in their mid-twenties approached and asked to play a game against them. Paul's friends were more than happy to be in the company of three attractive young women, so they ordered a round of drinks and began a game. The women were competitive and won the first game because their presence caused Kevin to become distracted, but they lost the second. When Paul called the waiter over to order more drinks, the women told them that unfortunately, they had to leave because they had to get up early the next morning. One woman walked up to Mike and offered him her number. Another insisted on giving hers to Paul; he was surprised when she spoke directly to him, and waited until he pulled his phone out of his pocket and rang her once to make sure he had gotten the number right. Afterwards, the women said goodnight and walked out the back door. Paul set up the table to play another round with his friends and ended up staying at the bar until almost midnight.

When Paul got home, he thought about what had occurred earlier that evening. He was pleased that the tall, pretty brunette, Monica had given him her number. It gave his damaged ego a momentary boost. Paul picked up his cellphone and noticed that her profile photo popped up on a messaging app he used frequently, so he sent her a chat message telling her that it was nice to have met her. She messaged back: *It was great to meet you too. Let's meet up next week.*

After his flirtatious message, Paul suddenly felt immense guilt. He didn't have a genuine interest in Monica. The only woman he cared for was Gabriella. Realizing how much she meant to him, he rang her to say hello and make excuses for why he hadn't called in awhile. Gabriella was friendly, but he could tell that she was struggling to understand his excuses. They spoke for several minutes longer, making polite conversation before hanging up.

Paul waited two weeks before calling Gabriella again. He had to finish some work and wanted it out of the way so that he could give her his full attention. When he called her on a Friday afternoon, she agreed to meet him for dinner that same evening. They decided to meet at a restaurant Paul knew Gabriella liked, but that he really couldn't afford anymore.

Paul arrived twenty minutes early to get the best table. As he sat waiting for Gabriella, he watched the entrance, anticipating her arrival. When she finally walked in, she looked stunning wearing a red shift-dress he had never seen before and high-heeled black boots; he guessed that her ensemble was from the new fall line at her boutique. As she approached, Paul felt like the luckiest man in the room. He rose to his feet when she reached the table and gave her a peck on the lips. His mood was lifted enormously just by being in her company. But it quickly dropped when he noticed her hostile body language. Taking a seat across from him, she picked up the menu and rather than look at it, flipped it over, laid it flat on the table, and began smoothing it down with both hands. It was an odd gesture that Paul had never seen before. Her mood seemed somber and formal, almost like someone at a funeral. Looking directly into his eyes, she said, "I rarely hear from you anymore. I thought you'd decided to end our relationship."

Paul stared at her open-mouthed, surprised by her statement. "Absolutely not. I feel terrible that you'd even think something like that," he responded.

Gabriella leaned towards him as if she were gossiping and didn't want others to overhear. A severe expression crossed her face as she spoke in a hushed tone. Her blonde hair nearly fell into the glass of water in front of her. "Paul, it's clear that you've lost interest. We barely see each other. This sort of thing is what I feared…an unstable situation."

Paul leaned back in his chair and took a moment to sort out his thoughts. "I've been going through a difficult time. It has nothing to do with you," he said, finally.

"I'm aware of your difficulties. We've discussed all

of that. But, that's not the issue I'm talking about," she said, curtly.

Paul looked at her blankly. "I don't understand."

Gabriella sat upright in her chair and began fiddling with the edges of the menu. She bent the top right corner with her fingers and glared at Paul. "Do you remember Anna, the girl who works at my boutique?"

Paul had no idea where Gabriella was leading their conversation, so he paused to think carefully before speaking. Assuming that she was referring to a student she had recently hired as a salesperson, he said, "Anna…Anna. Oh, yes. How is she?"

"She's fine. She saw you a couple of weeks ago playing pool at a sports bar. She hangs out at the same place you do, apparently. She said that you bought drinks for some women there, and you took their numbers."

Stunned, Paul didn't have a quick response to the accusation, so he tripped over his words as he considered the right comeback. "I didn't really…I mean...my friend Mike is single. He was with me that night. Maybe I took a number, but it was for him, not me."

"Why would you have to take a number for Mike? He's an adult. He knows how to take a woman's number by now, at least let's hope so. Something isn't right," Gabriella stated, flatly. Looking annoyed, she crossed her arms and leaned back in her chair.

Paul understood why Gabriella wanted answers, but at the same time he felt that she was overreacting. Realizing that he needed to find a way to steer the conversation away from where she was moving it, he decided to give her a simple explanation. "I'll tell you what happened," he said. "Three girls came over to our table. We were all surprised when they walked up to us. We had two short games of pool with them, and then they left. Nothing happened after that night. We only chatted with them the one time and never saw them again."

Gabriella moved her head sideways as if trying to gauge if Paul was telling the truth. "What you're telling me might be true and I'd like to believe you. But combined with the fact that you rarely call me, what other conclusion would I arrive at?"

"Gabriella, I'm only interested in you. I'm not seeing anyone else," Paul said.

Gabriella nodded and uncrossed her arms as if she wanted to give Paul the benefit of the doubt. She finally picked up the menu, turned it over, and began reading it. Paul didn't know what to say, so he began discussing the menu with her. Tired of being on the defensive, he was grateful that she allowed him to do this without further argument.

When the waiter arrived, he took their order and Paul allowed Gabriella to choose the wine, a chardonnay from Australia. As they waited for their starter, Paul went into a detailed explanation about his recent difficulties at his company and how he planned to deal with it all. Gabriella listened, gave him some suggestions, and then began to talk about her boutique and the boring task of taking inventory. The conversation remained polite and cordial throughout the rest of the evening.

After dinner, Gabriella didn't order tea like she normally did. She told Paul that she had to go home right away because the babysitter was leaving shortly. He had been hoping that he could talk her into coming over to his place for a couple of hours, but that fantasy was shattered. After Paul paid the bill, they spoke briefly about a mutual friend, and then Gabriella rose to take her leave. Paul stood up and then walked around the table to give her a kiss goodnight. Gabriella, rather than kiss him on the mouth, chose to kiss him on both cheeks which was completely out of character. He wanted to walk out of the restaurant with her, but got a strong vibe that she wanted to walk out alone. Feeling anxiety because of her coldness, he sat back down, took a sip of water, and watched her walk away. As Gabriella reached the exit, she quickly looked back at Paul, paused, and then rushed out the door.

Paul took another sip of water and looked over at the empty chair across from him. He noticed that Gabriella had left her napkin behind on her seat. Reaching over the table, he picked it up. Lifting it to his face he could smell her perfume. At that moment, anxiety overcame him, and he felt as if he had lost her.

The next morning, Paul hopped into his truck and drove out to the site where the homes he'd built were located. Having decided to add even more finishing touches to make them more appealing, he had been spending nearly every day there. Recalling Gabriella's behavior towards him the night before and wanting to fix things, he parked his truck and sent her a chat message, asking her how she was. He sat for fifteen minutes, patiently waiting for a response before stepping onto the pavement – but he never got one. "I screwed up, but she's making the wrong assumptions," Paul said, closing the door behind him.


Paul continued to contact Gabriella and she would occasionally accept his calls. But she would only speak with him briefly. Finally, he called her on a Sunday afternoon when he knew that she would be able to speak freely because her children were playing outside in the garden. Gabriella answered his call and was polite for the first few minutes, but soon after, their conversation took a negative turn. She told Paul that she wanted to remain friends, but felt that they should stop seeing each other romantically.

Paul was shocked by her carefully worded rejection. "What are you saying? Gabriella, please try and understand. I've been going crazy trying to deal with the situation I'm in. It has nothing to do with you. Don't do this."

Paul's pleas had no effect on Gabriella who had already made up her mind. "When I say we should remain friends, I truly mean it. At this time, I would just prefer to be alone," she said, softly, as if to lessen the blow. "I have to go now, Paul."

After his conversation with Gabriella, Paul felt like he had been shot. He stood in his living room, unable to move as if his feet had grown roots into the floor. A sudden weakness came over him and he lost his grip on his cellphone. Expecting it to crack apart and the battery to fly out as it fell onto the hardwood floor, he watched it simply drop sideways, as if in slow-motion, and then fall flat, making a loud thump. Although the sofa was only a few feet away, he felt too weak to walk over to it. He stood in total silence before lowering himself to the floor, and finally taking a seat next to his phone.

Paul felt more alone than ever before; his spirit was crushed, and his optimism gone. Gabriella's rejection felt like a weight holding him down. Lying back on a Persian rug, he stared up at the ceiling. Hours passed as he recalled the most precious moments of his relationship with Gabriella.

Paul finally snapped out of his trance when he noticed that the light coming through the windows had dimmed considerably, and guessed that it was early evening. Rising to his feet with difficulty, he walked towards the kitchen to get a glass of water. But once he reached the sink, he decided that water wasn't going to do the trick. He chose instead to mix himself a drink, pouring mostly vodka into his glass.

Paul walked back into the living room, sat down on the floor again, and knocked back his drink. As he rose to pour himself another, he heard his phone ring but decided to ignore it. A few minutes later, after he downed his second drink, it rang again, so he answered - it was Monica, the woman he had met playing pool. In his depressed state of mind, he spoke slowly and quietly to her. Monica noticed that he was speaking in a weird monotone voice, but since she hardly knew him, she figured he spoke that way normally.

"What are your plans for tonight? Do you want to meet up somewhere?" she asked.

"Unfortunately, I've had a couple of drinks and can't drive," Paul said, ice clanging in his glass as he swished around the remnants of his drink.

"It sounds like you've been having a good day," she said, laughing. "I'm with my friend Joanne. You met her the night we played pool."

"Yes, I remember her. How's she doing?" Paul said, feeling anti-social and trying to figure out a way to end the call politely.

"She's good. Right now, we're at Tony's Pizza. I don't know if you've heard of it. They make amazing

New York style pizzas. We could stop by your place and bring one over if you're not busy," Monica said.

Paul realized that he hadn't eaten for hours and had nothing left in the refrigerator. He doubted that he had the strength to drive his car to the grocery store, or the energy to jot down a list of items and request delivery. Also, if the women came over he wouldn't have to drink alone. "Alright. I mean, if it's not too much trouble."

"How far are you from where we met?" she asked.

Paul explained that he lived five miles away and gave Monica directions. He then changed his clothes and sat in a chair near the entryway so that he could hear their car pull up. By the time Monica and Joanne arrived, the alcohol had worn off and Paul felt that he was sober enough to entertain them. As he welcomed them in, he apologized for not taking them out and said that he would later that week if they were free. "Are you okay? You look exhausted," Joanne said, handing him two warm pizza boxes.

Paul didn't want to be a downer in the company of two beautiful women, so he ignored the comment. After inviting them to take a seat at the dining room table, he brought out plates, utensils, and napkins, and took a seat across from them. Opening the pizza boxes, he was pleasantly surprised to see that one was half-pepperoni and half-mushroom, his favorite combo, and the other, vegetarian. After finishing his first slice, he realized that there was nothing to drink on the table, so he went into the kitchen and came back with sodas and beer. As they ate their pizza, the women laughed and joked with each other, occasionally asking Paul questions about his house. They wondered why he didn't have a pet. "I only moved into this house recently. My dog died a year ago," he said.

Monica nearly dropped her second slice of pizza when Joanne unexpectedly nudged her with her elbow. "What? What's going on?" she said, annoyed with her friend.

Joanne pulled a barrette out of her handbag and used it to pin back her dishwater-blonde bangs. She then whispered something to Monica, and looked across the table at Paul, a concerned expression on her face. "Are you sure you're okay? You look depressed," she said.

"You're very perceptive," answered Paul. "I am depressed."

Monica looked up from her plate, curious to know what was bothering her new love interest. "Why?" she asked.

Paul pushed his plate aside and began to tell them about his business troubles. The women were sympathetic and listened intently. He then explained that earlier that day, his girlfriend had dumped him. "So, that's why I'm feeling down," he said.

"What was the reason she gave for breaking up with you?" asked Monica.

Paul didn't want to tell her that she was indirectly involved. "I'd stopped paying attention to her because I had to concentrate on my business and she assumed that I was cheating. Her ex-husband cheated on her, so she's hypersensitive."

"You mean paranoid," said Joanne.

"We were together for two years without any problems, so no, I wouldn't call it paranoia, but the actions of her ex-husband affected her, and she made some wrong assumptions about me. I'm guessing that she wanted to protect herself, so she hurt me before I could hurt her."

"She shut down emotionally," said Joanne. "I've done that myself, so I get it."

"It's definitely her loss," said Monica, glancing over at Joanne, who nodded in agreement.

Paul, suddenly feeling the loss of Gabriella acutely in the pit of his stomach, was unable to eat another slice of pizza. "Thank you. That's nice of you to say," he said, rising to his feet. Even though Joanne and Monica were kind and understanding, their presence made him feel more depressed. If he couldn't get Gabriella back he would have to date again, something he dreaded. These two young women were living, breathing reminders of what the experience would be like. Getting to know another person was never easy. "Would you like another beer?" he asked Monica.

"No, I'm fine," she replied.

"By the way, how much was the pizza? I'll reimburse you," said Paul, reaching into his back pocket and pulling out his wallet.

"Don't worry about it," Monica said, waving her hand dismissively.

Paul pulled some bills out of his wallet, walked over to Monica, and gently forced the cash into her hand. "You did me a favor. I probably wouldn't have eaten until tomorrow."

"Are you coming with us to the concert?" Joanne asked.

"What concert do you mean?"

Monica explained to Joanne that she had forgotten to invite Paul to the live music event they were attending that evening. Paul took no offense and said that he had heard about it but wasn't up for loud music. "I'll take a raincheck," he said, smiling.

Monica looked at her phone for the time. "I was hoping you'd give us a tour of your house, but if we're going to get a parking space, we'll have to leave now."

"No problem at all," Paul said, picking up their plates.

Monica and Joanne asked where the bathroom was and headed there together. When they walked back into the dining room, having applied more makeup, they looked completely different. "We'll be going now, but I'm going to check on you tomorrow to see how you are," Monica said, giving Paul a hug.

"Thanks for having us over," said Joanne, keeping her distance from Paul so that Monica wouldn't suspect her of competing for his attention.

Paul walked the woman to the door. "I look forward to hearing from you," he said.


Over the next three weeks, desperate to get Gabriella back, Paul left her countless voicemail and chat messages asking her to give him another chance, but Gabriella never responded. Worried that his behavior might be construed as obsession, Paul didn't want to seem like a stalker, so he chose not to stop by her boutique, although he drove by it sometimes to catch a glimpse of her inside. In his last chat message to her, he wrote: *Gabriella, I miss you. If we could just talk, we could straighten things out. Please get in touch with me.*

After another few weeks passed, Paul concluded that Gabriella didn't want to see him anymore and there was nothing he could do about it. What Paul knew for sure was that he had to pull himself up by his bootstraps, both financially and emotionally. He told himself that he was alone for now and had to accept it, but when he was ready he would start dating again. Once he made that deal with himself, he decided to focus on his financial problems, once again.

Paul had a friend whose business was buying up foreclosures. He would fix them up and rent them out, or sell them. Paul didn't like the idea of making money off other people's misery, so he chose not to become involved in foreclosures or sales, even though he was invited to join in that endeavor. Instead, his friend hired him as a contractor to renovate the properties he had bought. Paul got enough business to get by comfortably at first, but as the months passed and business kept rolling in, he started making a decent profit. Soon, he felt confident enough to begin dating again. Monica had contacted him on several occasions, but each time he'd politely declined. He didn't blame her for what happened with Gabriella, but she had been the catalyst for their breakup and was a reminder of his loss.

Paul has stopped driving past Gabriella's boutique to watch her inside. He has accepted that the relationship is over and doesn't think about her every day anymore. He is actively dating and feels ready for a new relationship.

## Steve's Breakup

At the age of twenty-five, Steve had earned a business degree and was now studying gemology so that he could work with his two older brothers, Brad and

Jonah, at their family-owned chain of jewelry stores. Steve's parents had passed away five years earlier and his brothers had carried on the business. Soon it would be his turn to join them as an equal.

Steve met his girlfriend, Mia, a twenty-eight-year-old college student working towards her Master's in Psychology when she entered a store run by his brother, Brad, one mile away from her campus. She walked in with her sister who had brought along her fiancé to look at engagement rings. The memory of when he first laid eyes on her popped into Steve's mind often. Mia was a stunner - her long golden-brown hair hung almost to her waist and her hazel eyes, the color of honey, warmly gazed back at him. Combined with her tanned complexion, she appeared golden all over. A slim but curvaceous woman of medium height, she had the ideal figure, in Steve's opinion. Mia had a Bohemian style and wore jewelry made of semiprecious stones such as aventurine and rose quartz. She took no interest in gemstones or designer jewelry and in the three years they had been together, she'd never asked Steve to bring her a gift from one of his brother's stores. Steve was grateful for her lack of interest because even with his wholesale discount, much of what was sold was expensive. Nevertheless, he had saved up to buy her something dazzling for her upcoming twenty-ninth birthday. Brad had set the necklace aside in his store so that once Steve finished paying it off, he could present her with it. It was a white gold lariat style, with a diamond in the center, and both sides ending in rubies. Steve knew that it was a chic item, but hoped that since the design was unusual it would be Bohemian enough for Mia. Buying it was Steve's way of showing her that their relationship was solid after they had broken up earlier in the year and then reconciled. When Mia had instigated their breakup, she told Steve that she cared for him but saw no future with someone his age and that she wanted to have a child by the age of thirty. But to his surprise and relief, one month later she called him to tell him how much she missed and loved him, and begged him to take her back. Steve, who had been miserable without her, took her back without argument, although he was honest with her and told her that he wasn't ready to settle down yet.

Even though things had stabilized between Mia and Steve, there was one nagging problem that affected their relationship negatively and hung like a dark cloud over his head. During the month that they were separated, Steve dropped by Brad's store one evening and found that he wasn't there. Rather than go home, he decided to stay after closing time, chatting with a new saleswoman Brad had hired, Jacqueline, an attractive woman in her mid-twenties. He had spoken with her several times before when he visited his brother and found her not only to be beautiful, but also intelligent and interesting; she was a highly competent salesperson and knew a great deal about gemstones. On that evening, while she was locking up the front of the store, something about the way she looked at him made him suspect that she was attracted to him. Feeling that he might be misreading her and deciding to make no assumptions, Steve went to the back of the store to find a tool to fix a watch. He had promised Brad the day before that he would repair it and was angry at himself for not having made it a priority. While he was standing in front of the work-desk holding the watch up to the light to make sure that he had fixed it correctly, Jacqueline walked up behind him. She asked him a question about the watch and then began speaking to him in a soft tone of voice. Unexpectedly, she stood in front of him, her back to the desk, and faced him directly. Placing the watch down on the desk, he stood still, confused by her actions. After making some flirtatious comments that were barely audible, she leaned against him in an obvious attempt to seduce him. Steve, who realized that his earlier observation had been correct, made no attempt to back away. Instead, he held her body against his and kissed her. Soon after, Jacqueline began unbuttoning her blouse but didn't get very far with it. Steve lifted her at the waist, set her down on the desk, and they had sex.

After their encounter, Jacqueline gave Steve her number, but didn't ask for his. When Steve drove home that night, he was nervous about what had occurred. Brad had strict rules about becoming romantically involved with employees and Steve knew that he had crossed a line. He avoided visiting his brother for days, but knowing that he would have to face the situation eventually, he walked into his store one afternoon to talk to him. When he saw the irritated look on Brad's face, Steve surmised that he knew the whole story. Luckily, Jacqueline was working at another store that day, so he didn't have to face them both. Once Brad finished helping customers, and the store had emptied out, Steve approached him as he stood behind the counter and apologized. "I'm so sorry about what happened with Jacqueline. How did you find out?"

Brad glared at Steve. "I overheard her on the phone the other day graphically describing everything that occurred to one of her friends. I came in the back entrance after lunch, so I snuck up on her without her knowing it."

"Did she know that you overheard her?"

"Yes, because when she turned around, I was standing there. You two did all of that on my desk? How could you?"

"It won't happen again. I promise," said Steve, looking down at his shoes, ashamed.

"It's okay though, because you're not the owner of a store yet. But once you have your own store, if an employee tries to seduce you, you can't allow it to happen. There could be legal ramifications depending on the circumstances," said Brad, sternly.

Although what happened made Steve feel embarrassed around Brad, the topic was eventually laid to rest. When Mia began calling him again, asking to get back together, Steve decided to put the incident behind him. Mia would have never found out if it weren't for a major slip-up on his part.

Three months after his encounter with Jacqueline, Steve sat on Mia's sofa in her apartment on a Friday evening, eating guacamole and chips, and downing tequila shots. After having one shot too many, he was beginning to feel the effects when Mia, who was standing in the kitchen several feet away, asked him offhandedly why he rarely visited Brad at his store anymore. "I'm embarrassed because of what happened between me and Jacqueline," he blurted out.

As soon as he let the words slip out he knew he had made a mistake. Eyes wide, he sat silently, praying that she hadn't heard what he said. Mia, who had been rinsing a glass, walked into the living room and sat down beside him. Her eyes welled with tears as she looked him, a shocked expression on her face. "You slept with someone else?"

143

"I said that?" said Steve, startled by Mia's quick reaction.

"Not exactly, but you inferred it," said Mia, angrily. "I know you – you're not likely to pick a fight with your brother's employee, especially one that pretty. So, the only other thing I can think of is that you slept with her."

Deciding not to lie to her, Steve explained what had happened and told her that it shouldn't count against him because they had been on a break from their relationship. Mia, enraged, walked over to the front door, threw it open wide, and demanded that he leave her apartment. Concerned he might say something that could make things even worse, Steve got up from the sofa and walked slowly towards the door. The room appeared to be moving sideways as he stood in the doorway, attempting to get her to calm down. When Mia shut her eyes and let out a loud sigh, he knew that the topic was closed, and that she had shut down emotionally, so he told her that he would leave, but would call her the next day. Or at least, that's what he thought he said. Knowing that he couldn't drive in his condition, when he reached the bottom of the stairs he called a taxi to take him home.

The morning after their argument, Steve stood in the shower feeling groggy from the tequila. His head pounding as the warm water fell over him, he thought he heard his cellphone ring. After wiping his hand on a towel, he picked it up off the sink and saw Mia's name displayed, so he hopped out to take the call. His plan was to apologize, but she spoke so quickly that he couldn't get a word in. "I just want to get some things straight with you. I understand that the opportunity presented itself when you and I were not speaking, and

I know why you couldn't resist. I've seen Jacqueline. She's that hot-looking brunette with the double D's," she said. "What worries me is that it could happen again."

Steve reached into the shower and turned the water off before grabbing a towel, and throwing it over his shoulders. "It will never happen again. I promise you," he said. "And anyway, Jacqueline has quit working for Brad. She's working for another company now. She left because she felt she could make more commission there."

"Please don't mention her name to me ever again," said Mia.

"I won't. But I just want to reiterate that she hit on me and not the other way around."

"Let's put it behind us. We won't discuss it again."

"Done," said Steve, hoping that she would keep her word.

Mia and Steve continued seeing each other and their relationship normalized, even though Mia, unable to contain her feelings of resentment towards Steve, made occasional digs at him for weeks over what she dubbed, "The Jacqueline incident." But soon, she acknowledged that indeed, they had been on a break from each other.

Knowing that Mia had final exams coming up, Steve gave her space so that she could concentrate on studying. This meant calling her a couple of times a week rather than every day. Steve knew that Mia regularly studied with a group of friends in the main library at her university and that she would likely be spending much of her time there. He had gone to dinner twice with her and one of the women in her study group named Haley, but she was the only close friend of Mia's he had ever met. Steve had to study for his courses too, but knowing that Mia wanted to be alone with her friends, he never asked her if she wanted to study together.

One afternoon, after taking a difficult exam, Mia met up with her friends in front of The Science and Engineering Building 2. Sarah, a slender brunette who hated Psychology and regretted taking it as a general course for credits showed up with Ali, a childhood friend of Mia's, and also a Psychology major. Haley, a blonde beauty who was taking some of the same classes as Mia because they were mandatory for the nursing program, showed up late, as usual. When everyone was accounted for, the women walked together over a grassy hill in the heat of the mid-day California sun towards the cafeteria.

As they entered the building, a blast of cold air caused them to shiver. Ali reached for the sweatshirt wrapped around her waist and pulled it over her head. "Damned that air conditioning system. I shouldn't have worn shorts today."

Mia and Haley, both on diets, stood in line at the salad bar, and Ali and Sarah walked over to an adjacent counter to order tacos. Mia picked up a plate and set it on a tray, but then realized that she didn't have an appetite, and placed them both back in their slots. "What's wrong with you?" asked Haley, grabbing Chinese chicken salad between metal tongs and setting it on her plate.

"I'll tell you when you sit down," Mia said. She turned her back on Haley abruptly, walked towards the middle of the cafeteria, and took a seat at a table for four.

Sarah was the first to pay for her tacos and soda. When she reached the table, she took a seat across from Mia. "What is going on?" she asked. She then picked up a taco and studied it, trying to figure out which end she should take her first bite.

Mia leaned forward, placing her elbows on the table. "Steve cheated on me a few months ago."

"Who did he sleep with?" Sarah asked. Haley unexpectedly popped up from behind, followed by Ali, causing Sarah to jump up out of her seat and nearly choke. Once they took their seats, she angrily threw a dirty crinkled napkin at Haley.

"A woman working at his brother's jewelry store, about a mile from here," said Mia.

"I remember you telling us that Steve was studying gemology. How many stores does your boyfriend's family own?" asked Ali.

"I think it's a chain of four or five," said Mia. "When he finishes with his studies he'll take over one of them."

"How did you find out that he cheated?" asked Sarah, poking at the ice cubes floating in her soda with her straw.

"We were having drinks at my place. I think he had too many, and it kind of slipped out."

"In vino veritas," said Ali.

"In tequila veritas," said Mia.

"Wait a minute. You told me about this awhile back," said Haley. "Don't you remember? You two were on a break from your relationship when it occurred. I can't believe this is such an issue that you're so upset you can't eat months later. And anyway, you're still with him."

Surprised by her friend's criticism, Mia paused to think carefully about how she would respond before speaking. "That's why I didn't break up with him again. It's true that we were on a break. But as time passes I'm feeling angrier and angrier about it. It really got under my skin. I didn't realize that until now."

Sarah nodded, indicating that she got Mia's point. "How did they hook up?" she asked.

"Where is the woman now? I mean…does he still see her all the time?" Ali interjected.

"No, he doesn't see her anymore. She quit and works somewhere else," Mia said, ignoring Sarah's question. "What bothers me is that she was drop dead gorgeous. I remember seeing her twice at the store when I went to meet him there. My boyfriend is only twenty-five, as you know. There's no way a young guy with all that testosterone isn't going to take whatever opportunity that comes his way. I'm thinking that a man in his mid-thirties or older would be a better match for me."

"You've said that before," said Haley. "But, remember Nick, my ex? He was forty-three and he cheated on me."

Ali and Sarah nodded in unison. "I don't think you should be ageist about this," said Ali.

"I just don't think he's right for me anymore. And recently when I've been out with him I've caught him looking out of the corner of his eye at other women," said Mia.

"You've never mentioned that before. It sounds to me like you're digging for excuses to end things with him again," said Haley.

"If you don't want to be with him anymore you should break up with him permanently. He's only twenty-five. He'll find someone else and move on. Maybe that would be the kindest thing to do," said Sarah, sliding her plate towards Mia. "Have a taco. I saved one for you."

Mia picked up the taco, but rather than eat it, she stared at it. "I have feelings for Steve," she said. "It should be that simple, but it's not."

Mia's birthday was coming up in a few days and Steve had finally paid off the necklace he planned to give her. He stopped by Brad's store on a Saturday evening to pick it up and saw that Brad had placed it in a beautiful midnight-blue velvet box. "She'll love it," he said, handing it to Steve.

Steve looked down at the box in his hands. "I spent all this money out of guilt because of what happened with Jacqueline."

Brad leaned against the jewelry counter, a severe look on his face. "You should have never told Mia. That was a mistake."

"I was drunk. But it's for the best that I was honest with her."

Brad shook his head in disagreement. "Honest about what? She didn't need to know. And if you think about it, she's lucky you took her back after she dumped you. What if the circumstances had been different, and you and Jacqueline had started seeing each other. If Mia tried to get you back, you wouldn't have been available."

"I'm certain now that Mia is going to be a permanent part of my life. I had to tell her the truth," said Steve.

Brad rolled his eyes. "I see that you're a lost cause, but I hope she likes the necklace."

When Steve got home he took a seat on the sofa and placed the necklace box on the coffee table in front of him. Feeling the sensation that it was burning a hole in the table, he thought about giving it to Mia before her birthday. He called her to drop the hint that he had bought her something. When she answered he asked her to put the call on video-mode so that he could see her. To his surprise, her response was cold. "Not today," she said.

"That's fine," he said, placing the phone on the table and tapping the speakerphone. "But you sound strange. Are you alright?"

"Steve, I have to tell you something," said Mia. "I can't get past the cheating incident."

Stunned, Steve's eyes widened. He had tolerated weeks of petty digs at his character, but felt certain that Mia had gotten over it. "I never cheated on you. We were on a break. You'd left me."

"I know I did, but you got over it quickly, didn't you?" she said, accusingly.

Steve recognized the hostile yet controlled tone in her voice from experience. He sat still, fearing the worst and praying silently that she wasn't about to break up with him again. "Mia, please just let it go. We agreed not to talk about it anymore."

"Look, you're young. You'll probably not get serious with anyone for a decade," she said.

"I'm serious about you," said Steve, frustrated.

"Haven't you noticed that my behavior has changed towards you. I've been distant ever since I found out you'd slept with that woman."

Steve picked the phone up off the table and began pacing, hoping it would help him think more clearly. "I noticed nothing after that one argument. You didn't change towards me at all."

"For me what you did was a horrible thing," she said.

"We've been together for three years. It happened only once, after you'd dumped me, and when you came back we agreed to drop the subject," said Steve, trying his best to rationalize with her.

"I tried very hard to get past it. I really did. But for me it's over and you'll have to accept it."

Steve stopped in his tracks. "Mia, you can't mean this. Don't break up with me again," he said, pleadingly.

"We're done. Accept it," she said, and then ended the call.

In a desperate attempt to reason with her, Steve called Mia back, but she didn't answer. His heart beating fast, he called Brad who answered immediately. "What's going on?" he asked.

"Mia broke up with me again. She told me it was because of my one-night stand with Jacqueline," said Steve, breathlessly.

"Are you sure it's not something else? A lot of time has passed."

Anxiety overwhelming him, Steve felt as if his heart was going to pop out of his chest. "She told me that was the reason, specifically. She also said that she wasn't fully in the relationship after that."

"She *was* fully in the relationship. As far as I saw, everything went back to normal," said Brad, perplexed.

"So, you didn't notice her behavior change either?"

"Something isn't right. My intuition is giving me signals that there's more to it than what she's telling you. Leave her alone for now. You have an exam coming up, so you'd better concentrate on that. Give her some breathing space," said Brad. "She came back before, so there's a chance she'll come back again."

"You think there's a possibility?" said Steve, his panic beginning to subside. "I'll leave her alone for a few days, in that case."

"Do that for now. Although she gave you a specific reason, I'm just not buying what she's saying."

"I've called her fifty times. She won't answer. When she broke up with me this time, I felt like she really wanted to cut me off permanently."

"Some women will simply stop calling you and no longer take your calls," said Brad. "You're lucky she came right out and said something rather than create a situation where the relationship slowly died."

"I don't feel lucky," said Steve. "I feel terrible."


The Monday morning after Mia broke up with Steve, he took a difficult gemology exam given online. After he finished and submitted it, he remained seated at his desk in his bedroom thinking about what to do for the rest of the day. A sudden feeling of loneliness hit him, and his mind immediately turned to Mia. Even though his attention had been diverted by his studies, the last couple of days he had felt so depressed that dragging himself out of bed in the morning had taken him over an hour.

Steve had never been a coffee drinker, but he recalled Brad telling him that he sometimes drank it throughout the day to give himself a pick-me-up. In a desperate attempt to lift his mood, he drank two cups that morning - and to his surprise it gave him energy, mental clarity, and a slight emotional boost. Believing that if two cups made him feel better, three cups would work even better, he made himself another cup. Unfortunately, it had the opposite effect and caused him to feel anxious. He felt so jittery that to rid himself of excess energy, he chose to go for a jog around his neighborhood.

When Steve returned home from his run, his mood had greatly improved. He decided that from now on, he would drink two cups of coffee and then go for a jog every morning. Feeling re-energized and oddly confident, he decided to confront Mia that day, in person. After changing into a pair of jeans that Mia once said were her favorite, and throwing on a t-shirt from a concert they had gone to together, he hopped into his car and drove to Mia's university. He guessed that she would likely be at the library studying with her friends, so he chose to go there first to look for her.

When Steve reached the university, he was unable to find a parking spot. Kicking himself for not realizing ahead of time that this would be an obvious problem, he parked almost a mile away. He walked briskly towards the library, going over in his mind every word that he would say to Mia. By the time he reached the entrance he was so exhausted that he bent over to catch his breath. Standing up again and composing himself, he walked past the librarian's desk and looked towards the back of the library. Sitting in a corner at a round table, he spotted Mia's friend, Haley. She was with another woman who had the same shade of golden-brown hair as Mia; she even resembled her slightly at a distance.

As he approached, Haley turned to look in his direction and squinted. Arriving at their table, he noticed two empty chairs and concluded that Mia was probably still in class. Upset with himself for not checking the time before bolting out the door, he said to Haley, "When will Mia be here?"

"She'll be in class for at least another hour," she said.

"Can I sit with you and wait for her?"

"Sure," said Haley, waving her hand over the chair next to her.

Steve sat down and then introduced himself to Ali. "I'm Steve. Have we met?"

Ali leaned across the table to shake his hand. "No, we haven't. I'm Ali, it's nice to meet you," she said quickly, before directing her attention back to typing on her laptop.

Steve turned to Haley. "Did Mia tell you that she broke up with me?"

Haley flattened her left hand and gestured in a downward motion for him to keep the volume down and said quietly, "Yes, I know about it."

"Do you think I have a chance at getting her back?" Steve whispered, leaning towards her.

Haley paused for a moment to think before speaking. "I thought you two were made for each other. But Mia has a timeline. She sees her life unfolding in a certain way and doesn't want to deviate from that."

"A timeline?" said Steve, scooting his chair closer to hers. "You mean, when she says that she wants to have her first child by the age of thirty?"

"Yes," said Haley. "She's heavily invested in the belief that she should have a traditional wedding and have at least two children within a certain time frame.

154

Many of her older sister's friends who never married because they were involved in their careers are having a hard time finding someone to settle down with in their thirties and forties, and regret that they didn't make it a priority earlier. I think talking to them influenced Mia."

"And she thinks because I'm young that I'm not committed to her? She told me that the first time she broke up with me. But this time she said she was breaking up with me because when we were on a break I had a one-night stand with another woman," said Steve.

"Your relationship with her is none of my business and I'm not going to pry or involve myself in your problems. But there doesn't have to be one reason for breaking up with someone – there can be several. I'm telling you this to explain to you why I believe she keeps breaking up with you, but I could be wrong."

"She thinks that she should be with someone thirty-five and not twenty-five. She sees no future with you," said Ali, looking up from her computer.

"She said those exact words?" said Steve, hoping that she would elaborate.

"She said something to that effect. But that way of thinking doesn't make sense. We think we can control life, but there are too many random things that can occur to mess up our plans. At least, that's my opinion," said Ali, looking over at Haley, who gave her a harsh look.

"So, you're saying that you think Mia is misguided in her thinking?" said Steve.

Haley and Ali both nodded. "I never want to get married," said Haley. "But, that could change. Whatever life has in store for me isn't written in stone."

"I'm not sure what I want. I just go with the flow," said Ali.

"Do you want to go with us to the cafeteria?" asked Haley. "We're going in about twenty minutes. They're having a special today on breakfast burritos."

Steve looked at Haley in disbelief. He couldn't get his girlfriend to speak with him, yet her closest friend had just invited him to breakfast. Worried that Mia might become even more distant and suspicious of him if he took Haley up on her offer, he said, "Breakfast burritos. Thanks for the invite, but I think I'll head home now. I'll call Mia later. Please let her know that I dropped by while she was in class."

"We'll tell her," said Haley. "I hope you two can work things out."

"I hope so too," he said, rising to his feet, and waving goodbye to Ali. Having less hope about fixing things with Mia but feeling better informed, Steve exited the library.

When Steve got home, he decided not to call Mia. Haley and Ali had verified what he had suspected all along – that she was rejecting him because of an idea in her head, rather than something he had done. Steve had seen Mia as his future wife but was ambivalent to make that sort of commitment yet. He wasn't sure how well he would be able to run his jewelry store once he was handed over the keys, and he didn't feel ready to be a father. He had told Mia often during their relationship that he was in it for the long run and that he loved her. But none of that mattered because her "timeline" apparently dictated her actions. Having more clarity about the situation, Steve decided to leave Mia alone for a while. It was still possible that she would come back like last time.

A month passed, and Mia never contacted Steve. Lying in bed on a Sunday morning, out of a strong desire to know more about her life without him, Steve picked up his cellphone and checked her profile on a messaging app he had often used to communicate with her, and what he saw shocked him. In Mia's profile photo she was standing next to a man in his early thirties; he was so good-looking in Steve's opinion, that he could have been an actor or male model. Steve noticed that he was slightly taller than Mia and could clearly make out his muscular physique under his suit. Upsetting him further was the fact that Mia was wearing a low-cut dress. Steve sat frozen, staring at the photo, when his friend Zachary suddenly messaged him on the same app.

Zach, a longtime friend of Steve's, coincidentally attended the same university as Mia. Weeks earlier, when Steve had messaged him about his discussion with Mia's friends, Haley and Ali, Zach mentioned that Ali lived in his neighborhood and that he was casually acquainted with her. He said that when he got a chance he would talk to her and find out more about what was going on with Mia, if she was willing to open up about her friend. Steve responded to Zach's message by asking him if he had gotten around to speaking with Ali yet. Zach wrote back that he hadn't run into her, but that he hoped he would soon. He then informed Steve that he had to go, but told him to hang in there and not be too depressed about the situation. Zach's sympathetic words gave Steve the strength he needed to finally get out of bed that morning.

During his morning shower, Steve accidentally used a body wash that Mia had left behind rather than his shampoo. The flowery scent was cloyingly sweet, but it was all he had left of her, so he rinsed it out slowly, trying to remember what it smelled like on her. Patting himself down quickly with a towel and wrapping it around his waist, he stepped out of the shower and decided to walk to the kitchen to make some coffee. After his second cup, Steve became nervous and was unable to control his curiosity any longer. He wondered if the man in the photo was the real reason why Mia had left him. He felt foolish that he had never thought of that possibility.

Setting his mug down on the counter, he picked up his cellphone, and began a chat with her. He wrote: *Who is the man standing next to you in your profile photo?* He then took a seat at the kitchen table and waited for a response. After twenty minutes, believing that she wasn't going to answer his question, he nearly jumped out of his chair when he saw a message pop up. Mia wrote: *He's my brother. We were at a friend's wedding last week. But really, it's none of your business anymore.*

Mia's curt answer stung Steve, but at the same time he was relieved that the man was her brother. He opened the photo again in his phone and made it larger so that he could see the man's features more clearly. When he saw a resemblance, he nodded, relieved. Mia had never lied to him before or cheated on him, as far as he knew, so he believed what she said.

Not wanting to argue with her, Steve chose not to ask her any further questions. Staring at his phone, he read her message several times in an attempt to read something positive between the lines - but there was nothing. Setting the phone back down on the table, he walked into the bathroom and looked in the mirror. The shock of seeing Mia with a man, even in a photo had been too much for him to take and when he looked at his reflection he saw visible signs of stress. Steve splashed his face with cool water and then walked into his bedroom. Sitting down on the bed he looked over at the pillows and recalled the nights he had spent with Mia. He dreaded the fact that he would never again have her in his bed. Determined to fight through his depression, he changed into shorts and a t-shirt, and went for a jog.

While jogging around his neighborhood, Steve wracked his brain trying to come up with a viable strategy for getting Mia back. It was clear that the ball was in her court, and judging from her chat message, it was evident that she was still feeling hostile towards him. He had considered showing up at her apartment but concluded that it would likely only make things worse. Besides, her building had a security buzzer downstairs and she would have to buzz him up, which she was unlikely to do. He'd made a mistake by starting a chat with her. If she had missed him at all and thought about contacting him, he had just set back that process by behaving in a jealous way. She knew that he was obsessing over her which gave her all the power and him none. When she broke up with him the first time and then later begged him to take her back, they'd had marathon sex over an entire weekend. Remembering that weekend vividly, Steve suddenly felt weak and had to stop jogging. He was used to having regular intimacy with her and didn't want to try and find someone else to fill that void in his life. Replace Mia? The thought was unfathomable.

Several weeks passed, and Steve still didn't hear from Mia. He regularly checked her app profile hoping to get a glimpse of what was going on in her life, but apparently, wanting to avoid another argument with him, she had recently posted a benign photo of pink roses. He also checked her social media accounts but there was little activity. She only maintained two accounts – one to connect with her family and the other was school related. The lack of information began to eat at Steve and he decided to contact Mia again.

On a Tuesday evening, while folding laundry on the floor in his living room, he picked up his cellphone and initiated a chat with her, writing: *I hope you're well. I miss you.*

Within seconds his phone indicated that he had received a response. Mia's message read: *Steve, I'm fine. Thanks for asking, but you need to go your own way. Forget me.*

Steve wrote back quickly: *Are you absolutely certain that you don't want to get back together?*

Steve's heart sank when he read Mia's response: *I'm 100% sure.*

Steve called Brad to tell him what had happened. "I'm not surprised," said Brad. "If she ever tries to get you back, I want you to promise me that you'll reject her. She's totally out of line. You did nothing wrong other than being born on a certain date and not wanting to marry before you're ready."

"So, what you're saying is that you think she might come back?"

"I hope not. But anything is possible."

"Should I try to sneak into her building and knock on her door?"

"Hell no! What I want you to do is remove Mia's number from your contacts list and please uninstall that app she uses. That way you won't see her profile pop up," said Brad.

"She's put up a random photo of flowers, so I can't see anything. But, I can't do that," said Steve. "I chat with Zach and other friends on it too."

"Then delete her contact details but keep the app. Months have gone by, don't you realize that? Mia broke up with you twice, not once. You've got to let her go. I know it hurts. I know you still love her. But she's giving you no choice. She's made up her mind. Don't you get that? Even if you got back together she would break up with you a third time," said Brad.

"I suppose you're right," said Steve, quietly.

"Send me a message when you've deleted her. And also, drop by anytime with the necklace you were going to give her. I'll give you your money back."

After hanging up the call with his brother, Steve wrote Mia's number on a piece of paper, folded it, and placed it inside a corner of his desk. He then scrolled down the contacts list in his cellphone and deleted Mia's details. After messaging Brad that he had done as he'd suggested, he checked the app and saw that Mia's profile was no longer there. All the evidence of his three-year relationship had disappeared in less than a second - if only the memories would too.

Six months after his breakup with Mia, Steve obtained his gemology certification. Confident that he was finally ready, his brothers allowed him to take charge of

161

a family store. Determined to make his store a success, Steve began working hard immediately.

But turning a profit wasn't as easy as he'd thought. He spoke with Brad and asked him what to do with items that didn't sell. Brad told him that if he was unable to move something at the store, he should sell it online at a discounted price. If the item still failed to sell, he should take new photos of it and try a different website. He also told him that in some situations it was best raise the price, which he claimed often worked. Steve listened intently and did what his brother suggested. It was good advice - Steve made money in his first year, unlike his brothers who claimed that they broke even when they started. Excited by his success, Steve suggested that they open more stores or even go national. But Brad shot the idea down telling him that it wasn't the right time. However, he said that since Steve had a business degree and was doing well, it was a plausible idea in the future.

In his second year in business, Steve worked just as hard, but soon he came to the realization that his life had no balance. He had become so involved in his business that he rarely socialized, and he hadn't dated at all since the breakup with Mia. After a busy Wednesday night at the store, Steve went home to unwind and check his online sales. After painstakingly adding more details under each item on the website, he decided to stop working for the day. Lying back on the sofa, he plotted new strategies for making more sales. But just as he shut his eyes and began to doze-off, he heard a notification on his phone. Thinking that it about an item that sold, he picked it up and saw that he had received a message on social media - it was from Ava, a woman he knew from one of his gemology classes. Her profile photo was too pixelated when he enlarged it to see her features clearly, but from memory he recalled what she looked like. A tall, athletic woman in her early thirties, she had the strong jawline of someone who was fit and worked out regularly. Her dark hair was cut in a Cleopatra style – shorter in back and slightly longer in front. Her eyes, the most memorable feature about her, were a marbled grayish-blue, and her lips, full and pouty, made her look younger. Her fair complexion contrasted with her hair, giving her an almost Gothic appearance. Ava had approached him after class and started a conversation on more than one occasion. But at the time, Steve had been too distracted by his problems with Mia and anxious about the responsibilities that came with owning his own store to pay her much attention. In Ava's message, she wrote that a mutual acquaintance had recently told her that he was running his own store successfully, and after hearing this, she'd decided to congratulate him.

Without putting much thought into his response, Steve thanked her for thinking of him. He then invited her to drop by anytime she wanted, and gave her the address of his store. He wrote that he was free for lunch the next day and if she came by around noon, they could have lunch together. Within seconds, Ava wrote back: *See you tomorrow.*


When Ava walked into Steve's store she looked the same as he remembered, except for the way she was dressed. She wasn't wearing her signature outfit of tight-fitting jeans, ankle boots, and a cardigan sweater over a tank top. Instead, she wore what he guessed was a yoga outfit. "Have you just come from a yoga class or the gym?" Steve asked, walking around the counter to greet her.

"No, but I'm going there later today," she said. "I don't know if I ever mentioned it to you, but I'm a personal trainer. I apologize if I look too causal, but I have a client at 2 o'clock and I didn't have time this morning to think about bringing a change of clothing."

Steve didn't mind – her outfit allowed him to see the curves of her figure. "Actually, this look is flattering on you. But I'm confused. Why did you study gemology?"

"My father is in the jewelry business and he wanted me to know something about gems. That's how I ended up in your class, but I prefer to remain a trainer," she said.

"In class I used to think that you were a model. You're so tall and slim," Steve said, noticing that they were the same height.

Ava stepped away from him as if he had insulted her rather than given her a complement. "I was never interested in modeling and people can't seem to understand that."

Realizing that he had offended her without meaning to, Steve changed the subject. "Would you like to go to a Thai restaurant? If not, there's a British pub around the corner."

"Let's go to the pub," said Ava. "We can have Thai next week."

"Alright, we can do that," said Steve, wondering why she wanted to make advanced plans with him before getting to know him better. As they walked down the street towards the pub, Steve looked over at Ava and felt an unexpected spark. Appearing to notice how he was looking at her, a coy expression crossed her face as she said, "And the week after that, we can plan something else."

Steve and Ava, feeling that they had a lot in common, began seeing each other. Ava's background in gems made it easy for Steve to communicate with her. Plus, both enjoyed sports and had similar taste in music. After a week of dating, they became intimate. To Ava, intimacy meant that they were a couple and she immediately began behaving as if they were in a committed relationship. Steve, not wanting to disrespect her and wishing to see more of her, allowed her to get close to him. To his surprise, Steve found himself in a satisfying new relationship. Nevertheless, he felt anxiety about their future together. Ava was six years older, and he worried that he would eventually get dumped again because of his age. One evening, while they sat together at Steve's kitchen table sharing pasta and a salad that she had made, she began talking about pesticides and why she preferred organic food, when he interrupted, and asked her how she felt about their age difference. He winced and started to panic when Ava stopped talking mid-sentence and looked at him, a strange expression on her face. But to his relief she began to laugh. "It's a good thing," she said, winking at him. "You've got stamina."

Once Steve felt that he and Ava were stable as a couple, he introduced her to Brad, and soon after, he took her out to dinner with his eldest brother, Jonah and his wife. Within a year, Steve and Ava's relationship had evolved into something neither had expected. They felt so connected and in sync that they often finished each other's sentences. But they maintained separate apartments because Ava refused to move in with a man without being married to him. However, she didn't pressure Steve to walk down the aisle with her.

On a Sunday evening, after dropping Ava off at her apartment, Steve's cellphone rang while he was driving home. Pulling over onto the side of the road, he saw a missed call and a chat message from his friend Zach - in it, he wrote that he wanted to tell him something about Mia. Steve was surprised by the effect that just seeing her name in writing had on him. His heart thumping in his chest, he put his car in park and answered Zach by starting a video call with him. When Zach answered, he held the phone directly in front of his face rather than at an angle like he usually did. Steve took this to mean that their conversation would be serious. "What's going on?" he asked.

"Not much," Zach said. "I just wanted to tell you something I found out today. Do you remember Ali? She's the girl who used to hang out with Mia in college...the one I told you that I knew."

"Yes, I remember her. She sort of looks like Mia."

"Correct. That's the girl. I just ran into her. A friend of mine injured his ankle playing volleyball and I took him to the emergency room earlier today. I ran into Ali there - she was with her mother who stepped on a rusty nail. Her parents are renovating their house and these things can happen, I guess," said Zach.

"That's got to be painful," said Steve. He desperately wanted to know what Zach had to tell him, but at the same time he had to mentally prepare himself, so he wanted the conversation to move forward at a slow pace.

"I'm sure it hurt badly. But there were people in the waiting room much worse off than her mother and my

166

friend, so we ended up sitting next to each other for over an hour and had time to chat."

"And she mentioned Mia, or did you ask about her?"

"She brought up Mia, not me. She told me about the time you came to the library looking for her. She said that you seemed upset, and she felt sorry for you. She also told me that Mia got married around two years back to a man she met at a party - a doctor, from Spain. They had a baby girl."

Steve's heart sank. Even though he was satisfied in his relationship with Ava, for reasons he couldn't explain, he felt jealous of Mia's husband. "That's what she always wanted – a husband and a baby by the time she turned thirty. It looks like she won," he said, defeated.

A confused expression crossed Zach's face. "Won what? Was there some sort of contest between you two?"

Steve shook his head. "I meant that she saw her life unfolding in that way. I'm happy for her. She got what she wanted," said Steve, trying his best not to show outward emotion.

Zach paused and blinked in rapid succession before answering. "No, you're way off. She got a raw deal out of that marriage. Her husband slept with another woman, left her, and moved back to Spain."

Steve looked at Zach in disbelief. This was the last thing he had expected to hear. "Are you serious?"

"Mia told Ali that she was thinking about contacting you. But I told her you were in a serious relationship and that she should probably tell Mia not to get in touch with you. Now I regret having opened my mouth. I'm so sorry. I'm such an idiot."

This was the opportunity Steve had dreamed of when he'd agonized over the breakup. Replaying what Zach said in his mind, he fell into a funk. He only snapped out of it when he heard Zach whistling at him in an attempt to get his attention. Finally, Steve responded. "What you said was the truth."

"So, you're not angry with me? It just slipped out."

Steve wasn't happy that his friend had made his decision for him, but he knew that Zach's intent wasn't malicious. The reality was that Mia had dumped him twice and had broken his heart badly the second time. He had fallen in love with Ava, but at the same time, had the strong desire to see Mia again, something that he knew wasn't in his best interest. His gut feeling told him that if he began speaking with Mia and she talked him into getting back together, it was likely that she would break up with him again, anyway. He would lose Ava over nothing. "I don't want to see her again," said Steve.

"Is it because she has a baby?"

Steve shook his head. "Not at all. I love kids. But it's not my child. It's the child of the man she married after dumping me," he said. "I wish her well. She told me that she has a large family and that they're nice people. I'm sure they'll look after her."

"I remember how much you loved Mia," said Zach.

"It was a painful breakup. But, like I said, what you told Ali was fine. I have to go now. We'll talk tomorrow."

"Just relax and don't think about it anymore," Zach said, before disconnecting.

Dazed after what he had just heard, Steve started up his car and drove home. For some strange reason, the drive, usually twenty minutes, felt like an hour. When he finally reached his apartment and entered, rather than wash up and change clothes, he sat on the floor of his living room fidgeting with his keys, thinking through everything Zach had said. It was then that it occurred to him to check the inside of his desk.

Steve made his way slowly to the bedroom and stood over his desk. Opening the top drawer, he began feeling along the corners inside and found the small piece of paper with Mia's number on it. Feeling a deep sense of loss, he pulled his cellphone out of his pocket and added her back to his contacts list. He watched as her profile photo popped up, like magic.

Taking a seat on his bed, he studied her photo. Mia was sitting outdoors on what he guessed were the wooden steps of her parent's front porch, looking down at a chubby, healthy baby, a serene expression on her face. Touching the screen of his phone to manipulate the photo, he made it larger to get a better look. The bright yellow dress she wore indicated to Steve that she was happy to be a mother. She looked exactly the same, only her long hair had been cut to her shoulders. Staring at the photo, a sense of calm came over him. He had rejected her in the end, something that seemed surreal to him. But at the same time, he knew that she had other things to think about. He was with Ava now, a woman who had never rejected him, and she didn't have a timeline either. Scrolling down his contacts list he removed Mia's details from his phone. Once again, she disappeared from his life.

# Aiden's Breakup

Aiden, a thirty-four-year-old casting agent working for a casting company in New York City, finally felt that he was in a good place in his life and was optimistic about the future. Originally from Florida, he had moved to Manhattan at the age of twenty after dropping out of college because he was unsure of what major he wanted to study and didn't want to be saddled with student loans. He lived what he often jokingly described as an "aimless life" for many years after his arrival, working in catering and as a bartender. At the age of twenty-eight, while serving hors d'oeuvres at a black-tie event, he struck up a conversation with a well-known character-actor who told him about a casting company he heard was hiring. "You don't need a degree for that," he said, and handed Aiden their business card. Aiden kept the card in his wallet for a week without looking at it, but on a whim decided to apply for a casting position online. And, to his surprise, he got the job. It wasn't until a year later that he found out the actor he had spoken to was starring in a major blockbuster - by writing on the form that they were friends, it gave him the clout he needed to obtain the position. But even so, he was offered a low-level job, and at first felt like he had made a bad decision. The money he made bartending and serving at parties was decent and he kicked himself for walking away from work that covered his rent sufficiently. Nevertheless, he stuck with it and within a year the casting agents above him saw that he had an eye for talent – this allowed him to rise quickly through the ranks. He was now one of four people making important casting decisions and earning what he felt was a good living.

Aiden met his girlfriend of two years, Kristine, when she came to a casting call with her friend Maria, an actress who auditioned frequently, but had difficulty booking work. A beautiful blonde in her mid-twenties, she came across as confident and witty. After finishing college, she began working as an intern at Christie's auction house and was later able to obtain a full-time position. Aiden loved Kristine and felt that she was the ideal woman for him. He was considering proposing marriage to her, but had put it off for a specific reason – he had been offered a job at a casting company in Los Angeles that would pay him nearly double what he was making in New York. He knew that if he moved to the West Coast he would be in a long-distance relationship with her unless he could talk her into coming along with him. Knowing that she was happy working in Manhattan and had most of her friends and family there, Aiden felt that it was a tricky situation, so he hadn't told her yet. The company that approached him said that they wanted him, specifically. However, if he didn't accept the job, it would eventually go to someone else. They were giving him three months to make up his mind. Tired of putting off telling Kristine, Aiden decided that he would discuss the situation with her at the start of the upcoming weekend.

After work, on Friday evening, Aiden called Kristine to ask her if she would like to have dinner at an Argentinean steakhouse near her office. "Sure, I love that place," said Kristine. "But can we go to the bar first? They make excellent martinis. I can be there in an hour."

That evening, after exiting the subway station, Aiden walked quickly towards the restaurant, aware that he would be arriving later than he had expected. Kristine had a good sense of time, so he knew that she would be waiting for him. When Aiden entered the bar area he saw Kristine leaning against a barstool in the back, laughing with the bartender. As he walked towards her he saw two men to his left in their mid-thirties standing a few feet away, looking at Kristine and speaking in hushed tones; it was clear to Aiden that they were deciding how best to approach her. Feeling lucky to have walked in at that moment, he sat down next to her and said a friendly hello to the bartender. Kristine smiled and gave him a peck on the lips. "I ordered you a beer," she said, handing him the ice-cold bottle. "The bartender is new. He's from South Carolina. He made me this drink. It's called a 'Red Wedding.' It's my second one. Would you like to try it?"

"No, thanks. Beer is fine. Do you want to stay here, or would you like to find a booth?" he asked.

"Let's find a booth," she said.

Aiden paid the bar bill and grabbed Kristine's hand. She followed behind him trying to hold her drink steady as they walked through the restaurant. "You're already tipsy?" Aiden said, noticing that she was stumbling as she walked.

"My heels are hard to walk in," she replied, sounding annoyed by what she considered an accusation.

Once they reached an empty booth, Aiden gestured to a passing waiter that they wanted to sit there. When the waiter nodded that it was okay, they took a seat inside the c-shaped booth. Aiden placed his beer in the

172

middle of the table and looked over at Kristine who did the same with her drink, mimicking him.

Aiden turned to his right and saw that the two men who had been ogling Kristine earlier were no longer looking at her. He wondered if she had taken notice of them, but chose not to ask. Kristine sat silently, seeming to know that Aiden had something important to say. "I want to talk to you about something. I'm not sure what to do," said Aiden.

Kristine looked at Aiden inquisitively, and then folded her hands in front of her on the table. "I figured that there was some sort of problem," she said. "I could tell by your tone of voice."

Aiden grabbed his beer and took his first sip before speaking. "Two weeks ago, I was offered a job in LA. The pay is nearly double. It's a good opportunity and I want to accept it, but I don't want to be separated from you. I've never been in a long-distance relationship before, but from what I've heard they rarely work out. I was hoping that you might consider moving out to LA with me."

Kristine looked down at her hands and paused for a moment, a severe expression on her face. "I can't go to Los Angeles. My friends, my family, and my job are all here. I'm not even sure that I would like LA."

Although he had expected her to say that she preferred to stay in New York, he was stung by not just the negativity of her words, but also the pessimistic tone in her voice. He thought that she might protest, but since Christie's had an office in Los Angeles, he had hoped that she would have at least considered making the move. Trying a different tack, he said, "You'd be starting a new life there with me. Of course, we would be settling down together."

Kristine beamed at Aiden. "You want to get married? I've been waiting for so long to hear you say that." she said. But just seconds later, a sour expression crossed her face. "But now that you're moving to LA, it doesn't seem possible."

"I didn't say that I was moving there. I just said that I had a job offer."

"Yes, but you want to take it."

"I do, but I can see now that it would ruin everything."

Kristine picked up her drink and peered into it. "You don't like your job here?"

"I do," said Aiden. "But I can't move up to a higher level, so I can't earn more than what I'm getting now. I suppose I could apply somewhere else in New York, but things are cliquish here and it's hard to get on the inside. I suppose I could give it a try, though. Why don't I do that, and we can talk about something else."

"But you still want to marry me?" she said, smiling.

"Yes, but let's hold off on it awhile. I want to figure out what to do about my work situation first."

"I understand," said Kristine. "I won't pressure you."

Aiden grabbed a menu and looked at the long list of entrees. Kristine's blunt rejection of his plan caused him to lose his appetite. He decided to order something light, rather than one of the succulent steaks that usually tempted him.


A week after Aiden brought up the touchy subject of moving to Los Angeles with Kristine, he made it a priority to actively look for work in Manhattan. The problem was that most people in the industry knew each other or were connected in some way socially, and gossip spread quickly. The company he worked for could easily find out that he was searching elsewhere for employment if he wasn't careful. Concerned about this, when he applied for jobs he used his mother's last name instead of his father's hoping that it would offer him some anonymity. Unfortunately, this was an ineffective, and soon after, Shelly, his boss, called him into her office to ask him why he was looking for another job. Sitting next to her on her plush, purple velvet sofa, he explained that he had been offered a good position in Los Angeles, but that he didn't really want to move to the West Coast.

"I was shocked when I heard that you weren't happy," she said, her coffee mug wobbling in her hand.

"That's not the case at all, Shelly," he said. "I love coming to work. What happened was…a company in LA offered me double."

Shelly, a former actress, now in her sixties, had spent time in Los Angeles in her youth. She'd returned home to New York after a failed affair with a married producer when she was in her forties. The mess that followed destroyed her career as an actress and she'd had to rebuild her reputation in New York. Aiden guessed that because of her negative experience, she had become hostile towards the industry people in Los Angeles. After placing her coffee mug down on the floor, something she never did, Shelly pulled a black hair twisty off her wrist and wound it around her flaming red hair, creating a ponytail at the nape of her neck. Her purple glasses slipped down the tip of her nose as she turned to look him in the eye. "They offered you double?"

"Yes."

"I heard you got an offer from Ross Miller of Miller & Stevens Casting, but I'm surprised that he's willing to do that. Maybe it's because of his dislike for me," she said.

"I had no idea you knew Miller," Aiden said, astonished that she knew exactly who it was that had offered him the job. He hadn't told anyone other than Kristine, so he could only guess that she had heard it from an old contact living in Los Angeles.

"I think you should accept it. You're young and the pay is fantastic."

"I would take it, but like I said, I don't want to move to LA," said Aiden.

"Why not?" she said, flatly. "It sounds like a good deal."

Aiden noticed the confidence in Shelly's voice. If he left he could be replaced, so she wasn't going to try and stop him. "My girlfriend refuses to move there. I have to stay in New York."

Shelly nodded. "That explains why you were pounding the pavement here. Miller whet your appetite and you thought that you could pull off getting double here."

"I was testing the waters," he said, quietly.

"Once you establish a life out there, your girl will follow. I'm certain of it. She won't find someone like you easily – handsome, intelligent, and kindhearted. Not in Manhattan. It's simply not possible. There are more women than men here – it's a competitive dating environment."

"So, you're letting me go?"

"I'm doing you a favor," she said. "I don't want to hold you back. We're friends and we'll remain friends."

"Yes, of course," said Aiden.

"Now, go and get ready to start your new life. I'm meeting with Melinda now for a reading."

Rising to his feet, Aiden leaned over to give Shelly a hug goodbye before exiting her office. Walking home in a daze, Aiden thought about his situation - with no job and no prospects, he had no choice but to move to Los Angeles. When he reached home, first he called Ross Miller, and then Kristine to tell her what had happened.

"Shelly heard through the grapevine, so there was nothing you could have done," said Kristine.

"Once I'm settled, I'll fly back to see you often. We'll spend weekends together. We'll work things out. I promise you."

When Aiden finished his conversation with Kristine, he thought about all the changes in his life that he would now have to deal with. He had lived in New York for over a decade and had only been to Los Angeles twice for meetings. The thought of moving to a city on the opposite side of the country was scary – he would have to adjust to the culture in LA quickly. It was then that he realized that asking Kristine to uproot her life because he had spoken of marriage had been wrong-headed. He couldn't undo what he had done, but Kristine sounded supportive. There was still a possibility that she would join him, so he decided to move forward methodically with his plans and not dwell on the negative aspects of the situation. Aiden picked up his cellphone and searched online for moving companies. He had told Miller that he would be in LA within three weeks, and he planned to keep his word.

* * *

Within a week of moving to Los Angeles, Aiden was fully aware that he had entered a completely different world. The dress code at the office was more relaxed, but he found the work environment to be competitive and hostile. Nepotism was endemic, and when he made casting decisions that he thought were correct, he was often castigated for hiring people who he felt had genuine talent rather than the family member or love interest of an insider. In New York, when making casting decisions, strong skills were the most important factor because the intent of the casting director was not only to cast well, but also to build long-term relationships with talent. Actors competed with one another for roles in the theater, so their skills were more varied. One afternoon, Aiden approached Miller after a casting session to discuss this issue. He and his partner, Mary Stevens, were sitting together in front of a long white desk drinking organic tea out of paper cups, discussing the private schools they planned to send their children to, when Aiden pulled up a chair across from them. "I'm having a hard time casting people who I consider weak actors," he said.

Miller and Stevens looked at each other and nodded as if they had expected him to come to that conclusion. "You're coming from New York where you were also involved in theater casting and that's why we wanted you on board with us. Talent counts a great deal, but the offspring of the rich and famous have name recognition and pull, so we've been casting them more than we normally would have in the past. However, we're skeptical too, so we cast people who are truly gifted whenever we can," said Miller.

"Also, as you know, we now have offices in Atlanta, New Orleans, and Montreal," said Stevens. "Casting is national, and also more international than ever before, so we have a large pool of talent to choose from. We spend more time looking at self-taped auditions than having in-person interactions. I know that New York is more social, but hopefully, you'll get used to how things are done here. By the way, how do you like the house?"

"It's spacious and nicer than I expected," said Aiden. While still in New York, Miller's assistant had called to inform him that she had found him a furnished two-bedroom house to rent not far from the casting office. It had a pool and a large kitchen, luxuries Aiden was unaccustomed to, and the rent was only slightly more than what he had been paying in Manhattan for a one-bedroom apartment. Impressed by the photos she sent, he had accepted it. When he moved in, he took pictures with his cellphone of each room plus the pool and sent them to Kristine in a chat message. She wrote back that she was excited about the pool and claimed that she approved of the décor of the house, but said nothing about wanting to move to Los Angeles. Deciding not to pressure her, Aiden felt that if she missed him enough she might stop by human resources at Christie's and inquire about a job on the West Coast. In the meantime, he would continue trying to get used to his new surroundings.

After three months of maintaining continuous, almost daily contact with Kristine, Aiden decided   to fly out to New York for a weekend trip to surprise her for their upcoming two-year anniversary. While checking flights online, he recalled their first date and how she had been confused by a green Cymbidium orchid bouquet he had bought for her. It was the first time he had ever bought flowers for a woman other than for Valentine's Day, but he felt compelled to buy them for Kristine. When she opened her door and welcomed him in, she looked at the bouquet and said, "You brought me vegetables. How nice."

Enjoying her sense of humor and knowing that she was sentimental, Aiden decided to buy her the exact same bouquet. He called the flower shop in Manhattan to make sure that they had the orchids in stock. He then booked his flight and called his friend, Nick, who he planned to stay with, to tell him what time his plane would be landing. Nick and his live-in girlfriend, Chloe, used to double-date with Aiden and Kristine. But during the time that Aiden was in Los Angeles their relationship ended. Chloe continued to contact Nick, telling him that she wanted to remain friends. Nick took her calls because he believed that she already had regrets about leaving him and was sure that she would return soon. Since the breakup, Nick had been living alone and was glad to have Aiden for company.

Keeping the trip a secret had been difficult. Aiden considered Kristine his confidante and told her about most things that were going on in his life. She always gave him her valuable input and offered her support in clever and amusing ways. Before boarding his flight, Aiden sent Kristine a casual chat message, but gave no indication that he would be dropping by her apartment that evening.

When Aiden's flight landed at JFK Airport, he hopped into a taxi that took him to Nick's apartment. The flight had been over five hours, and by the time he arrived at Nick's door he was tired. Noticing this, Nick suggested he wait until the next day to see Kristine. "It's three hours ahead here. Did you forget that?" he said. "Look at your phone. It's after 11 o'clock. By the time you get to her place it will be midnight."

"I wanted to bring her flowers, but I can do that tomorrow, I guess," said Aiden.

"You could, if you wanted. I doubt that she would care whether you brought her something or not. She would be happy just to see you," said Nick.

Aiden decided that his friend was right and planned instead to drop by Kristine's apartment the next morning at 10 a.m. when he knew she would be awake, drinking coffee and reading the news online in front of her laptop as she always did. Nick said goodnight to Aiden and gave him his privacy so that he could unpack in the living room, and get some sleep on the sofa. To Aiden's relief, Nick's sofa was firm and comfortable, but he wouldn't have minded sleeping on the floor if it he'd had to because he preferred spending time with his friend to being alone in a hotel room. After setting the alarm on his cellphone, Aiden fell into a deep sleep.

Aiden awoke the next morning at 9 a.m. to the sound of his phone alarm and heard Nick's voice coming from his bedroom, begging him to turn it off. "Sorry," shouted Aiden. "I just wanted to make sure that I got up on time."

"No worries," Nick shouted back.

Aiden showered quickly and then dressed. He didn't shave because Kristine had told him in the past that she liked how he looked with five o'clock shadow. While hopping into a taxi, he realized that he hadn't eaten anything in over twelve hours. He felt lightheaded, but he would be at Kristine's apartment soon and could eat there.

When Aiden arrived at Kristine's building, he ran quickly up the stairs to the third floor. He knew that the peephole on her door was cracked, so when he reached her doorstep he stood close to the door, hoping she could make out that it was him. He rang the doorbell and waited for her, but when she didn't respond he put his ear to the door. That's when he thought he heard the voice of a man and woman speaking inside. Believing that he might be mistaken, he knocked on the door until Kristine finally opened it. Oddly, she kept the chain on - it was a long chain and he could see six inches inside. Standing bleary-eyed in front of him, she said, "Aiden? Why are you here? What's going on?"

Aiden walked towards her, but she stood frozen and didn't remove the chain. Noticing that something was wrong he backed away. "Are you alright? Are you sick?" he asked, concerned.

"I'm not sick," she said, turning her head around to look behind her. "I didn't expect you to be in New York."

Just as Aiden was about to explain that he was there to surprise her for their anniversary, a man's arm encircled Kristine's waist. Aiden could see that he was wearing boxers and no shirt. Stunned, Aiden stepped back, tripping over his own feet, and fell against the wall. He continued staring, trying to figure out if he was having a bad dream or that what he was seeing before his eyes was really happening, when the man said, "Is he the guy in the photos you showed me?"

"He's the one," she said, quietly. "He lives in LA."

As he looked at Aiden, a sympathetic expression crossed his face. "I'll leave you two alone to talk," he said. Letting go of her waist, he turned and walked towards the kitchen.

Aiden stared at Kristine, eyes wide. Her actions had rendered him speechless. Noticing this, she said, "I'm so sorry. I don't know what to say."

Once he was steadily back on his feet, Aiden began moving slowly towards Kristine. He wanted to enter the apartment so that he could see her bedroom, the place where she had betrayed him. And he wanted to speak with the man to make sure with absolute certainty that she had cheated on him of her own free will and not because she had gone to a party, had too much to drink, and ended up in bed with him. He had to believe that she had been manipulated or seduced when she wasn't thinking clearly. When he reached the door and pushed on it, Kristine panicked and slammed the door in his face. "It's our anniversary today," he shouted. "That's why I came here. I wanted to surprise you, and instead this is what I see."

He heard faint footsteps come close to the door and saw the shadow of her legs underneath it. "I didn't mean for this to happen," she said.

"This is what's been going on all this time? Every day you were lying to me? Why?"

"I wasn't lying," she said, softly.

"Do you even know this guy?" he asked, banging on the door with his fist.

"I don't know what to do," she said, sobbing.

Behind him, Aiden heard a door open. He turned around and saw an elderly man in a bathrobe standing in his doorway, looking at him angrily, as if the noise in the hallway had woken him up. "What's going on? Is everything alright?" the man asked.

"I just found my girlfriend in bed with another man," he said.

"That's bad," the man said, and quickly closed his door.

Doubting that she would open the door to face him again, and fighting his anger, he headed down the stairs. As he stepped onto the sidewalk, it began to rain. Rather than walk back into Kristine's building until it lightened up, Aiden chose to stand in the middle of the sidewalk, allowing the rain to fall upon him. To him, it was if the sky was representing the feelings that he had yet to express. The shock and disappointment of what he had seen overwhelmed him to the point where he felt numb. When he had first seen Kristine through the door chain, he had become aroused. But when he saw the man standing behind her and realized what she had done, he felt revulsion. The pitying look on the man's face made it even worse - with the picture of his arm around Kristine's waist embedded in his mind, Aiden decided to walk away from her building as fast as he could, and as he did, the droplets of rain that fell upon him began to feel heavier and colder. He then realized then that he had forgotten to bring his jacket with him. In Los Angeles he had rarely needed one, but this was New York – it surprised him how quickly he had adjusted to the warm weather there. Deciding to step under an awning in front of a jewelry store, he pulled his cellphone out of his pocket and called Nick, who answered immediately. "If you forgot your wallet here and need me to bring it to you, you'll have to wait at least half an hour. I'm not up yet," he said.

"I didn't leave anything behind," said Aiden. "I caught Kristine with someone else."

"You what? I don't understand."

"I knocked on her door. She opened it. And she was with a man."

"Maybe it was her brother or a neighbor."

"He was in his boxers, and touching her," Aiden said.

Nick paused as he tried to comprehend what he had just been told. "I can't believe it!" he finally said. "I don't know what to say."

Aiden stood listening to Nick ramble on about how surprised he was and how no one in their social circle would have ever expected something like that to happen. After several minutes of this, Aiden interrupted him. "I'm coming back now. I'm walking, so it will take me awhile to reach you."

"Take a taxi. I can see that it's raining from my window. I'll leave the door open for you since you don't have a key," said Nick. "And Aiden, although I know this is the last thing you ever expected to happen, it's best that you found out now. It could have gone on a lot longer."

Aiden stopped in his tracks. Nick was right – Kristine could have duped him for months and he would have been none the wiser. "I agree. I'll be there soon," he said, ending the call. Aiden took long strides as he walked, but when he was just two blocks from Nick's apartment, instead of the confident feeling of anger, he suddenly felt an overwhelming sadness wash over him. Tears welling up in his eyes, he leaned against the wall of a building and cried. He had just experienced the ultimate betrayal - Kristine, the woman who he had wanted to marry and spend his life with had done something horrible that he never saw coming. He wondered if he had ever known her at all. Having just witnessed her callous and cowardly behavior, he realized that it was possible he had been lied to before and never figured it out. It wasn't until a young woman in a trench coat approached and asked if he needed help that he became aware of his public meltdown. Thanking her for her concern and telling her that he was fine, he wiped his eyes and ran the rest of the way to Nick's apartment.

Aiden had originally planned to stay in New York until Tuesday so that he could spend time with Kristine. But because circumstances had changed, he saw no reason to miss an extra day of work, and changed his flight to Monday morning.

Thanking Nick for his hospitality as he exited his apartment, Aiden noticed the downcast expression on his friend's face. "I know how upset you were when Chloe moved out. You probably wanted to talk about it. And all I did was talk about myself," said Aiden.

"I'm upset about it, but she keeps calling me. She might come back," said Nick.

"You're sure of that," said Aiden.

"Yes," said Nick. "Don't worry about me. Whatever happened between us was nothing like what you're going through."

On Aiden's flight back to Los Angeles, he watched movies and tried to keep his mind off Kristine as much as possible. Once he arrived home, he unpacked quickly and then pulled his cellphone out of his pocket to see if anyone had tried to contact him. There were two missed calls from the casting office and one from Nick.

Wanting to thank him again for being such a good friend, Aiden called Nick back before checking in with the office. When Nick answered, he spoke so quickly that Aiden couldn't get a word in. "I'm getting ready to meet some friends now, but I'll briefly tell you what happened today," he said. "Chloe called me this afternoon and I told her what happened between you and Kristine. I'm sorry I told her, but it turned out to have been a wise thing to do. Chloe gave me some information that you should know."

Aiden pulled open the sliding glass door that led to the pool and walked outside. The incident with Kristine, which he'd barely had time to process, was apparently already being talked about amongst his friends. Looking at the glittering sunlight reflecting off the pool, he took a seat on a lounge chair, knowing that the news he was about to hear was likely to upset him further. "Go ahead and tell me," he said.

"Chloe told me that the man you saw must have been Kristine's ex-boyfriend from five years back. She said that she saw them out together two weeks ago at a restaurant. They were waiting for a table at the bar."

Aiden thought that the story already sounded credible – Kristine always liked to hang out in restaurant bars before dinner. "So, it's an old relationship that's been rekindled," said Aiden. He doubted that Kristine had been ecstatic about him leaving so that she could go out and pick up other men. It made sense to him that one of her exes would take advantage of his absence to try and get her back.

"When Chloe walked up to Kristine to say hello, she got the impression that they were an old couple and thought it was strange, so she rang her the next day to get the full story."

"If she'd picked him up at a bar because she was lonely that would have made me feel better. That way I could have forgiven her, and we could have put this behind us, possibly," said Aiden.

"Unfortunately, that's not the case. You can call Chloe if you'd like, but she'll tell you the same thing."

Aiden nodded and looked up at the cloudless sky. "Did Kristine say that he was her boyfriend and I was out of the picture?"

"She implied it. When Chloe asked if you'd broken up with her, she said that you hadn't, but since you'd moved to a different city, she considered your relationship to be over. Apparently, he's in finance and recently divorced. He began calling Kristine right after you left."

"So basically, she left me and simply chose not to inform me."

"It looks that way," said Nick. "But she was honest when she told you that she didn't want to move to LA. Maybe you should have seen it coming."

"How was she able to pretend like nothing had changed and that we were still together? I had no clue what was going on."

"Maybe she didn't want to lose you because she wasn't sure that it would work out with him. And you were always good to her. She would have no reason to dump you."

"She's a very talented actress. She's better than 90% of the people showing up at my casting calls," said Aiden.

Nick laughed. "I'll bet."

Aiden breathed in deeply and exhaled. Realizing that Nick was right and that he had probably ignored warning signs, he thanked him for the information.

After ending the call, he remained seated on the lounge chair, and watched the sun begin set. Finally rising to his feet, he walked back into the house and entered the kitchen. He felt physically weak, emotionally drained, and utterly disappointed by how things ended with Kristine. After pouring himself a glass of wine, he rang his colleagues back and then decided to watch horror movies for the rest of the day. Although often ridiculous, this film genre always reminded him that life could be a lot worse. At least he wasn't possessed by a demon or being chased by hungry zombies.

Aiden went to work early Tuesday morning as planned, even though he had hardly slept. He ran on adrenaline during the rest of the week, and because he lacked an appetite, he rarely sat down to eat a meal. He found it both interesting and disturbing that whatever he ate seemed to have little or no flavor. Even green tea, his favorite hot drink, tasted like a cup of nothingness. He wondered how long it would take for his taste buds to recover from what happened in New York.

By mid-afternoon on Friday, after having suffered insomnia for days, exhaustion finally set in. Aiden could no longer concentrate on what he was doing and suspected that his body was worn out. Worried that his co-workers might notice how tired he was and feeling that it would be risky to drive home, he left work two hours early. Leaving his car in the parking lot, he walked down the street to a four-star hotel and checked in.

Upon entering his room, he turned down the air conditioner to a tolerable level and removed his blazer.

Images of what occurred in New York continued to go through his mind. But these thoughts, that had haunted him all week were not enough to keep him awake any longer. He was so tired that he'd hardly been able to string a sentence together at the reception desk and felt lucky that he had been given a room key. Lying down on the bed, he went to sleep.

Aiden awoke the next day at 6 a.m., according to the digital clock on the glossy black guest phone on the bedside table. This meant that he had slept for a full fifteen hours. Feeling strangely warm, he rose from the bed, walked over to the air conditioning unit, and turned it higher before entering the bathroom. Looking in the mirror, he barely recognized himself; his bloodshot eyes and chalky-looking complexion were proof of the hell he had put his body through. He had been so zonked out that he'd fallen asleep in his clothes. Looking down at his shirt, he noticed that two buttons had popped off and vowed to find them. Removing his clothes, he left them in a heap on the floor and hopped into the shower. Thinking about what he planned to do that day, he decided that he would order a large breakfast before going home. He wondered if the fact that he was feeling hungry meant that he was beginning to feel better, but then concluded that he was simply running on empty and needed to refuel.

Exiting the bathroom carrying his clothes, a surge of cold air hit him. He was sure that he would catch a cold from the air conditioning, something he couldn't afford to happen. He had important casting decisions to make on Monday and knew that he had to be in a peak state mentally and physically so that he made no mistakes. Aiden slipped back into his boxers, put on his trousers and undershirt, and then called room service. After ordering a continental breakfast, he requested an iron. While waiting for both to arrive, he noticed the sun shining underneath the curtains of the dark room. Walking in the direction of the sliver of light, he pressed a button on the side of the wall to open them. Sun flowed in, shocking his senses and causing him to squint. Once his vision normalized, he opened the sliding glass door and stepped onto the balcony. Taking in the beauty of the trees and flowers below and breathing in the crisp morning air, he decided to remain outside. Looking down, he saw two white chairs facing each other at a low table. The fact that there were two and not one reminded him that he was alone. He recalled a similar set of chairs on the balcony of a hotel room he had shared with Kristine a year earlier on a trip they'd taken to Miami. He wished she was there with him now, drinking coffee and smiling up at him. No longer able to enjoy the beauty of his surroundings because of the flood of memories, he changed his mind and chose to have breakfast inside the room instead. Attempting to distract himself, he turned on the television and began searching for his missing buttons.

Several weeks passed before Aiden's friends in New York began sending him chat messages, telling him how sorry they were about his breakup. The wording of the messages reminded him of condolence cards. Early on a Sunday evening, while he was home sitting in front of his computer doing work, another message popped up on his phone. Tired of the onslaught of depressing messages, he considered ignoring it, but then decided to look once more. Picking up his phone, he saw that it was a message from Kristine. Feeling anxious, he tapped the screen. It read: *Aiden, I hope you're doing well in LA. I miss you and think about you all the time. I feel terrible about what happened.*

Aiden responded*: I heard through friends that you're getting serious with your ex-boyfriend from five years ago.*

Kristine answered: *That's not true. We aren't serious.*

"But she's still seeing him," said Aiden, shaking his head. He wrote*: I wanted to marry you. Does he?*

Aiden looked down at his cellphone, but there was no response, so he began working again. An hour passed and then two before he knew with certainty that she wasn't going to write him back. Unable to control the desire to get the whole story out of her, he called her, but she didn't answer. While waiting to see if she would respond eventually to his missed calls, he rang Nick for emotional support. Nick didn't sound surprised to hear from him. "Chloe told me that Kristine was going to call you. Did she?"

"No, she messaged me a weak attempt at an apology," said Aiden, laying his phone back down on the desk and placing the call on speakerphone. "I called her, but she didn't answer."

"I think it's not working out with that guy. She might be trying to get you back."

"If that was the case she would have answered my calls, but she's being a coward. Anyway, it no longer matters. I can't get the vision of that guy groping her out of my head," said Aiden. "I no longer trust her. And the memory of her slamming the door in my face won't leave me either."

"Maybe she thought that you were doing the same thing and hooking up with other women," suggested Nick.

"Do you really believe she thought that? You know me. I'm loyal. I was in constant contact with her."

"So, what are you going to do now? Are you going to start dating women in LA and forget about Kristine?"

Aiden sighed. "I have to put her behind me. But I'm not sure that dating now would be a good idea. With the kind of luck that I've had lately, I feel pretty pessimistic."

"What was the name of the woman you dated before meeting Kristine? I can't remember," said Nick.

Aiden grabbed a pen and began twirling it in his hand. "Her name was Amber. We dated for six months. I found out that she was seeing someone else behind my back, but I didn't catch her in the same way I caught Kristine."

"She was a party-girl though, wasn't she?" said Nick. "That was kind of a no-brainer. Kristine was more conservative. You can't compare the two."

"No, but both cheated on me," replied Aiden.

"And now, you're disillusioned."

Aiden ran a hand through his hair and leaned back in his chair. "That's an understatement." Not wanting to discuss dating anymore, Aiden told Nick that he had to run some errands and ended the call. Wanting to get his mind off Kristine's semi-apology, he read over some documents and afterwards, went to the gym.

By the early summer, Aiden began to enjoy his job. He became friendly with some of his colleagues and began going to parties with them. At a party hosted by Karen

Alberts, an old friend of Miller's in her mid-sixties who ran her own casting company, it dawned on Aiden that he was one of the few men there who wasn't paired off with a date. As he stood in the garden drinking champagne with friends, Karen approached him and gave him a hug. "I have a gorgeous friend I'd like you to meet," she said. "Follow me and I'll introduce you to her."

Although he felt uncomfortable, Aiden didn't want to be rude and decline the offer, so he allowed Karen to hook her arm around his and guide him over to the bar a few feet away. Aiden immediately understood why she used the term "gorgeous" when she stopped in front of a tall brunette in her twenties. The woman wore a feminine white dress and was struggling to remain upright on the grass in her wedge-heels. She looked at him and smiled politely. "I'm Isabel. You must be Aiden," she said, putting her hand forward to shake his.

Aiden smiled back at the woman and shook her hand. At that moment, as if she had done her good deed for the day, Karen dropped his arm and walked behind the bar to check how much alcohol was left. She then quickly approached another couple and began speaking with them. Feeling awkward that he had suddenly been left alone with Isabel, Aiden couldn't think of anything to say. Seeming to sense his shyness, Isabel spoke first. "I'm an actress. Maybe Karen didn't tell you that."

"What have you worked on recently?" he asked, trying to make casual conversation. As she answered his question, he noticed that her large eyes, almost black, were the exact same color as her long wavy hair. She wore a transparent pale-pink lip gloss that he found sexy. Her medium-pitch voice was pleasant and melodious, causing him to relax in her company. But although he found her attractive, he had no interest in her. Trying to force a spark that wasn't there, he glanced over her slim figure, his eyes resting on her bust. Noticing this, she giggled and rolled her eyes at him. "My eyes are up here," she said, pointing to her face.

Embarrassed, Aiden said nothing and directed his attention back to her face. He stood listening intently to what she told him about a project she was working on and occasionally interjected his opinion about the writer or director. As he continued to listen to Isabel's perspective on her work, Aiden suddenly felt depressed. Unable to focus further on their conversation, he felt the need to calm his nerves with a drink. Abruptly excusing himself, he walked over to the bar and ordered a cocktail. Downing it while still standing in front of the bartender, he asked for another, stronger drink. Knowing that he had already made a mistake with Isabel and that two drinks in his system would likely only make things worse, he walked past her and approached a group of his co-workers sitting at a table. Immersed in their conversation, they hardly noticed him as he took a seat. Taking a sip of water from a glass that wasn't his, he tried to bring himself back to a state of equilibrium. He looked over at Isabel – she was already talking to another man and didn't seem to care that he had disappeared. Sitting next to him was his friend from the office, Jay, who was downing shots. Assuming that Aiden was looking in his direction because he wanted some too, Jay placed four shot glasses in front of him. Tempted to escape his depressed state of mind, Aiden accepted the challenge.

By the time Aiden downed his fourth shot he began feeling nauseous and called a time-out with Jay, explaining that he had stupidly mixed his drinks, and had very little in his stomach. Deciding to find the bathroom in case his nausea got worse, he stood up and zigzagged his way towards the house. When he entered, he walked in the wrong direction and found himself in the kitchen. He then made another wrong turn and found himself standing in an open room full of books shelves that he guessed was either an office or study. Turning on a lamp, he walked towards the center of the room. Enjoying the peacefulness and quiet, he chose to stay there awhile and take a break from the party. To his right, he saw an old-fashioned brown leather recliner. It reminded him of the chair his father used to sit in when he was a child back in Florida. Taking a seat in it, he pulled the side-lever that lifted his feet. Grateful that the nausea had subsided but feeling heavily sedated after having far too many drinks, he shut his eyes and rested.

Aiden awoke to the sound of a tiny dog yelping. Opening his eyes slowly, he looked down and saw a fluffy white Pomeranian, barking underneath his feet. Standing above the dog was Karen wearing a modern beige kimono-style robe and slippers looking down at him. After initially being surprised to see her, he realized that he had never left her house. Looking over at the window, he saw light coming through the blinds and guessed that it was morning. "I didn't want to disturb you last night," she said. "You were out cold. I actually took your pulse to see if you were alive."

"I'm so sorry. This has never happened before," he said, struggling to stand.

"You're a wreck," she said, shaking her head pityingly. She leaned over and pressed down the side-lever of the chair; slowly the leg lift went back to its original position. "You were sitting on the remote. Didn't you feel it?"

"You mean for the chair? I did, actually," said Aiden.

"I'll make you some coffee and drive you home."

"No, it's okay. I can drive. I'll be fine."

Karen shook her head. "You can barely stand, so how are you going to drive?"

Aiden straightened his posture as best he could. "I couldn't find the bathroom last night. I guess that's how I ended up in here. I got lost."

Karen pointed towards the hallway and said, "It's in the middle of the hallway. It's a small guest bathroom, so I understand how you could have missed it."

Following Karen's directions, Aiden found the bathroom and washed up. Stepping out into the hallway, he heard dishes clanging and followed the sound to the kitchen. There, he found Karen standing next to the sink, her dog jumping around her legs excitedly. Aiden approached and then crouched down to pet the dog. When he stood up, she handed him a cup of coffee and smiled kindly at him. "This blend is strong," she said.

Aiden took the cup from her hand. "I'm embarrassed. I don't drink much usually. I don't know how this happened."

"I think I know," she said. "You're not ready."

Aiden peered into the dark liquid that was his coffee. "I don't understand."

"I heard from Miller's assistant, Elizabeth about what happened to you. She told me that you caught your fiancée in bed with another man a few weeks ago."

Aiden recalled a brief conversation he'd had with Elizabeth about failed relationships. When he told her the story of what had happened to him, she was shocked. He wasn't angry that she had told Karen, but he wished he'd known before he came to the party. "Elizabeth had been unceremoniously dumped by her boyfriend," he said. "I was trying to explain to her that she wasn't alone."

"I know," she said, lifting the cover of a sugar jar sitting on the kitchen counter and sliding it towards him.

Aiden took a spoonful and stirred it into his coffee. He then reached for the creamer and poured a small amount into his cup. "I can never escape gossip," he said. "New York was just as bad."

"I could tell you stories that would really depress you. But I'm not going to do that," she said.
Picking up her dog, she turned and walked down the hallway. A few minutes later, she returned wearing a red hat and blouse, and a pair or white jeans.

Aiden, finished with his coffee, placed the mug in the sink. "I'll just leave it there," he said.

"Are you ready?" she asked pointing towards the front door. Aiden nodded that he was and followed her outside to her car, a sleek white convertible Mercedes. He hopped inside, noting how comfortable the seat was.

As Karen backed out of the driveway he saw his car parked in a corner next to the gate and placed a hand in his pocket, feeling for his keys. Thankfully, they were there. "I'll come back later today and move that out of your way," he said.

"No rush. You can pick it up tomorrow or anytime. When Stan died I sold his cars, so there's plenty of space."

As they drove down Sunset Boulevard, the warmth of the sun beamed down upon them, cutting through the coolness of the morning air. Every time the car came to a stop at a traffic light, Aiden felt a pleasant breeze. "I'm doing better, but sometimes I can't sleep and I feel so tired all of the time. I think it's due to depression," said Aiden, looking over at Karen. "I hope I wasn't rude to your friend. What was her name again?"

"Isabel, but don't worry about it. Like I said earlier, you aren't ready to start dating again. Anyway, the weather is fantastic, as usual," she said, smiling.

Aiden sat quietly, enjoying the sun and the breeze. He had a lot to be thankful for – he made a good living at a job he enjoyed, his social life was improving, and he was getting over Kristine even though it was a slow process. The romantic spark that he hadn't felt for Isabel would come again sooner or later. And when it did, he would be ready for it.

# Chapter Sixteen

## Reconditioning Yourself to Dating

After a failed relationship, you might feel war weary, like you've fought hard but lost the battle. It's not easy to get back out there and try again. If you're out of practice because you've just come out of a long relationship, dating can be intimidating. You're putting your ego on the line, hoping for a mutual attraction with someone you find desirable. At the same time, you're wary whenever you meet someone new. Even if things go well, changes take place and adjustments need to be made in your life to make room for this person. Not everyone can do this with ease. If you're not quite ready, take your time and gradually start going out more. Be open to meeting women, but don't make it your number one priority. Go out and have fun with friends or by yourself.

## Have Patience and Reasonable Expectations

When choosing a partner, their physical appearance counts of course, but you shouldn't limit yourself by sticking to a particular "type" only. Do you tend to reject women who you don't feel an instant attraction to? If this is your dating pattern, keep in mind that real love takes time to develop. Passionate romances that occur quickly often burn out just as quickly. Don't expect a woman to rock your world when you first meet her. When you like someone as a person and enjoy her company, a spark might come later. Being patient has its rewards. A slow growing romance that starts with friendship can lead to an exciting, passionate relationship.

## Never Waste Your Time

It's never wise to invest all your energy in a woman who gives you conflicting signals or behaves in a hot and cold manner. Unless the relationship stabilizes and she makes a solid commitment, keep your options open and date other women. If you continue to date someone exclusively and put your heart and soul into the relationship, but are not getting equal interest in return, you're only wasting your time - eventually you'll kick yourself for having stayed in an unsatisfying relationship that wasn't tangible or stable.

## Getting Over Disappointment and Trust Issues

For some, the disappointment of being betrayed or losing the affections of someone they love is so great that they are unable to bounce back and date again. They would rather be alone than potentially put themselves through the trauma of another heartbreak. These feelings are understandable. However, when this becomes your attitude, what you're doing is giving the person who hurt you the power to destroy your trust in people. The world is full of quality women who will not betray you, and are trustworthy and kind. But if you don't allow them access you'll never come to that realization. To counter trust issues, get to know a woman slowly.

Remember to always look for someone who is a genuinely good person. Ignoring signs that a woman has bad character and continuing to date her is foolish. Recognizing and appreciating good character will make your dating life a hundred times easier, and allow you to meet an all-around great person.

## Using Dating Sites

A great way to meet women is through friends, at a party with people you know, or even through work because you at least have some background on them. Another good way is to hang out in your neighborhood – at the gym, a coffeehouse, local event, or even the grocery store. But if you feel that you're not meeting enough women in your daily life, you might want to try dating sites. What's wonderful about these sites is that you don't have to build up the courage to walk up to a woman who is surrounded by friends at a party or worry that her boyfriend might approach you from behind and inform you that she's with him. Women are on these sites because it makes meeting people easier for them too, and they don't have to get dolled-up constantly to try and meet men at events or nightclubs. Most women on these sites want a relationship and not a hookup, so you can find a potential marriage partner this way.

One of the downsides of dating sites is that they give people the perception that they have never- ending choices, so they often feel little empathy towards people they interact with. Also, when looking at profiles, people tend to judge others mainly on their appearance. The problem with this is that some people are more adept at photographing themselves than others – they know about lighting and angles – so a beautiful woman might take a photo that makes her look less attractive than she is, and visa versa. It can be difficult to gauge your attraction to someone who is not standing in front of you, so you might choose wrongly and miss the opportunity to meet someone that in real life you would find interesting. Another problem is that people tend to set parameters that limit them – you might state in your profile that you want to meet a woman who is within a certain age range and miss out on meeting someone that happens to be a bit older or younger who you might have had more in common with. Dating sites are sometimes used by women who are not seriously looking to meet men in order to boost their egos, or to keep men they contact as backups if things don't work out in their current relationship. However, this is rare.

The vast majority of women are genuinely looking for a relationship.

If you decide to delve into this way of meeting women, keep in mind that most people have good days and bad days while utilizing these sites. If you don't like the way one site operates, try another. If you're concerned that the person you wish to meet might be different than what you were hoping for, you can always plan a quick video call before setting up a formal date to make sure that both of you have the desire to move forward.

You can walk away altogether and stop using dating sites if they make you uncomfortable. Most people still meet their significant others in traditional ways, even though the number of people using dating sites continues to grow. Meeting someone online works for people who are very driven to find someone, and who can accept rejection as well as reject others without becoming anxious during the process.

## Approach Attractive Women When the Chance Arises

One of the reasons that people ping-pong in and out of low-quality relationships with their exes is because they don't actively try to meet new people. Shyness and the fear of being rejected or misunderstood are the main causes. It's difficult to break this negative pattern of thinking, but it can be done.

Learn to pay attention to your surroundings when you're out of the house doing errands, going to and from work, or wherever else you find yourself frequently, rather than staring into your cellphone.

Once you are aware of what's going on around you, you'll notice people more, including women who you might find attractive. The old techniques of being chivalrous, charming, and masculine still work like charms on women – people have become so accustomed to staring into screens that they've forgotten these basics. If you find yourself in a coffeehouse and see an attractive woman you'd like to meet, if she appears interested, you can casually comment on what she's drinking, or invite her to take a seat next to you, and strike up a conversation. If you're at the gym, you can ask a woman when she'll be done using the treadmill. If she finds you attractive, she'll smile at you or otherwise indicate that she's glad you spoke to her - she will then automatically lengthen the conversation. That's your cue to hand her your business card or ask her if she's willing to give you her contact details. Don't miss the opportunity to meet someone because you saw a hot-looking woman on social media or a dating site and you think she might go out with you. What's in front of you is better than the unknown.

Don't worry if you don't look like Adonis. Women are much less visual than men and they often view quirks and imperfections as sexy or cute. A gorgeous man can turn ugly quickly to a woman if he comes across as self-centered or rude. But a man who is chivalrous, polite, and friendly will make a woman feel safe and view him in a positive light. Behaving this way doesn't mean that you're a "nice guy" who will end up being used as a doormat. It means that you respect yourself, you respect her, and you have an honor code that you abide by in all situations.

If you get shot down, don't worry about it. You can try again another day. Some women will find you charming, and others will have a negative transference to you. That's just how life is, so don't allow the fear of rejection to perturb you from speaking to women. A woman's body language and facial expression will indicate whether you should buy her a cup of coffee or walk in the opposite direction.

## Avoid Discussing Your Ex on a Date

During the dating process, a woman will usually ask a man about his dating history. This helps her figure out if he is emotionally stable, is dating casually, or is looking for something serious. If you find yourself in this situation, there's nothing wrong with giving a woman a very brief overview of the relationships you've had that impacted your life. Make sure to sound diplomatic and neutral when discussing your exes, especially the one that devastated you the most and broke your heart. You can simply tell your date, for example, that you recently came out of a two-year relationship, and in your opinion, it failed because you both had work pressures. There's no need to elaborate or re-open wounds. And never use foul language when discussing your exes. Even if you have a hundred reasons to be hostile, don't show these feelings to the new woman you're dating. It might cause her to assume that if she began a romantic relationship with you, that you would speak badly of her if things didn't work out. Keep it classy and come across as strong and confident. If you end up in a new long-term relationship, and the woman in your life continues to bring up the topic of your past relationships, you can give her a few more details to assuage her curiosity. Or, even better, you can tell her that the past is irrelevant and that she is your present and future.

## Luck in Romance

Luck in romance can be achieved by being optimistic and confident. You need to be able to put yourself out there. If you get hurt or experience a setback, it's important to believe that it's only temporary and that luck will swing back in your favor. Improving romantic luck involves:

- Being upbeat and positive.
- Not harping on mistakes you feel you've made in your relationships. Try to avoid making the same mistakes in the future, but stop replaying them in your head endlessly.
- Looking forward to tomorrow's opportunities.
- Actively trying to meet someone. You've got to be out there and available.
- Focusing on your strong points, not your weaknesses.
- Not allowing cultural beliefs to cripple you. Keep those beliefs that have helped you, and distance yourself from ways of thinking that have always worked against you.
- Accepting some risk in life. If you plan every detail you leave no room for luck. Luck involves some uncertainty…some volatility.

207

- Being willing to win or lose. If you don't try, you'll never know what the possibilities are.
- Wearing clothes that look good on you and make you feel great.
- Being around people and making connections.
- Spending time with optimistic and successful people who see the possibilities in life.

# Breakup Survival
# Summaries

- If you've just come out of a long-term relationship you might feel out of practice when it comes to dating. Start by being more social.
- Don't put all your energy into someone who gives you mixed signals or doesn't have an equal interest in developing a healthy, stable relationship.
- Don't let disappointment and trust issues keep you from dating. But don't rush into a new romantic relationship; take your time getting to know someone.
- If you enjoy a woman's company and are interested but not extremely attracted to her, try being patient and allowing a slow romance to develop. If it does that's great and if it doesn't, then so be it.
- Remember to always look for good character in a woman.
- Romantic luck will come with positive thinking and action.
- If you haven't had the best luck lately, consider it temporary. You'll be lucky again.

Hopefully, after you've finished reading this book you'll be on your way to achieving your goal of getting over your breakup. And when you do, know that you have a world of options and wonderful things can happen for you. By remaining positive you can never lose.

**About the Author:**

Susanna Gold is a writer whose main focus is love, romance, dating, and relationships. She divides her time between Los Angeles and London.